The *Tourist*
TRAVEL & FIELD GUIDE TO THE
Ngorongoro
CONSERVATION AREA

Written by
Veronica Roodt
Published by Veronica Roodt Publications
2006

Published by Veronica Roodt Publications
PO Box 367, Hartebeespoort, 0216, Republic of South Africa

First published - 2005
Second edition - 2006

Written by **Veronica Roodt**
Printed by: House of Print: Tel (+27) (11) 493-8516 (Johannesburg, South Africa)

Photographs: All photographs and illustrations by **Veronica Roodt** except where
otherwise indicated by acknowledgment next to photo.

Distributed in South Africa by:
Veronica Roodt Publications
   Tel/Fax: (+27) (12) 253-2883 (Pretoria, South Africa)
   Email: vericon@mweb.co.za
   Mobile: (+27) (0) 72 634 9415
   Website: www.veronicaroodt.co.za or www.africamaps.co.za
Veronica Roodt Distributors
   Tel/Fax: (+27) (12) 549-1355 (Pretoria, South Africa)
   Mobile: (+27) (0) 72 316 9712
   Email: veronicaroodt@lantic.net

Distribured in Tanzania by:
Veronica Roodt Publications (see details above)
Ngorongoro Conservation Area Authority (NCAA)
   Tel (Arusha): +255 27 250-3339 or 254-4625
   Tel (Ngorongoro): +255 27 253-7019 / 7006 / 7046
   Fax (Arusha): +255 27 254-8752
   Fax (Ngorongoro): +255 27 253-7007
   E-mail: ncaa_faru@cybernet.co.tz or ncaa_info@cybernet.co.tz
   or ncaa-info@africaonline.co tz
   Website: www.ngorongoro-crater-africa.org
Kase Stores
   Tel: (+255) (27) 250-2640
   Fax: (+255) (27) 254-8980
   Mobile: (+255) (0) 744-380-222
   Email: kasestores@habari.co.tz

In order to improve and update the book and map, feedback is welcome.
Please contact Veronica Roodt at address: PO Box 365, Hartbeespoort, 0216
or email: vericon@mweb.co.za or tel/fax: (+27) (12) 253-2883.

ISBN 0-620-34191-2

PREFACE

The aim of any map, travel guide or field guide book is to improve the tourist's experience by offering concise, accurate and easy-to-use information. Weight and space restrictions often limit the number of books one can carry. It thus made sense to combine detailed maps, travel information and a photographic field guide into one publication. This book consists of the following:

- **Maps** - A map of Tanzania, the NCA and 12 detailed satellite maps of all tourist areas.
- **Travel information** - The first section consists of a travel guide with information on how to get there, where to stay, road conditions, best season to visit and climate.
- **Background information** - It includes detailed information on the history, people, topography, geology, hydrology and archaeology.
- **Field guide** - The second part of the book consist of information and photographs of over 500 plants, animals, birds, reptiles, amphibians and insects.
- **Contact details** - Contact details for hotels and lodges in the general area and safari companies operating from Arusha are provided at the back of the book.
- **Index** - A comprehensive index for easy reference is at the back of the book.

Hopefully this book will enhance the readers' experience and inspire more people to visit Ngorongoro - one of the most beautiful and unique natural phenomena left on earth.

Enjoy your visit!

ACKNOWLEDGMENTS

I would like to thank the Chief Conservator of the Ngorongoro Conservation Area, Mr Chausi, for allowing me to do this project and for his kind and friendly assistance throughout. I also want to thank Mr Murunya for co-ordinating everything and for all his help. My sincere appreciation to Mr Lazaro Ole Mariki for co-ordinating the fieldwork and especailly for his help with the editing and checking of the Maasai words. Then I want to thank Mr Stephen Lelo for providing some of the photographs and for his contribution in the editing of the book. Without the support of the above people, none of this would be possible.

A very sincere thanks to Mr Lenyatso July, who accompanied me on all the trips to Tanzania and who assisted with the tracking of the roads. I also want to thank Pieter Swart and Rob Kauzil for their input and Janine Fourie for her motivation, assistance and patience throughout the project.

Veronica Roodt

ABBREVIATIONS

Abbreviations used throughout the book:			
NCA	- Ngorongoro Conservation Area	SNP -	Serengeti National Park
NCAA	- Ngorongoro Conservation Area Authority	TANAPA -	Tanzania National Parks
		FZS -	Frankfurt Zoological Society

CONTENTS

MAP REFERENCES

COLOUR CODE REFERENCES

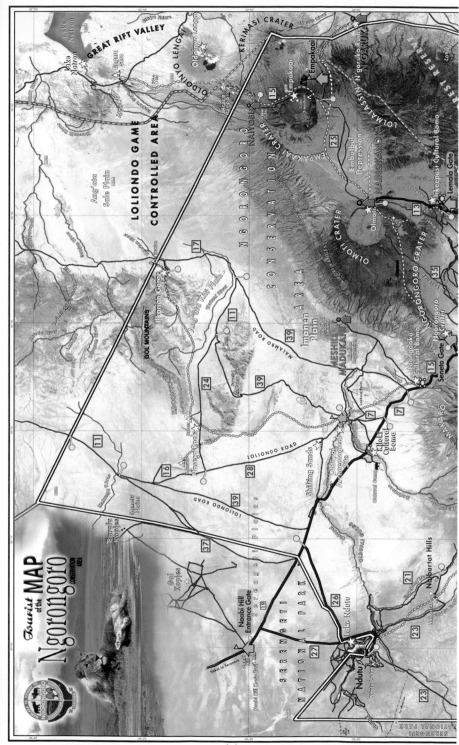

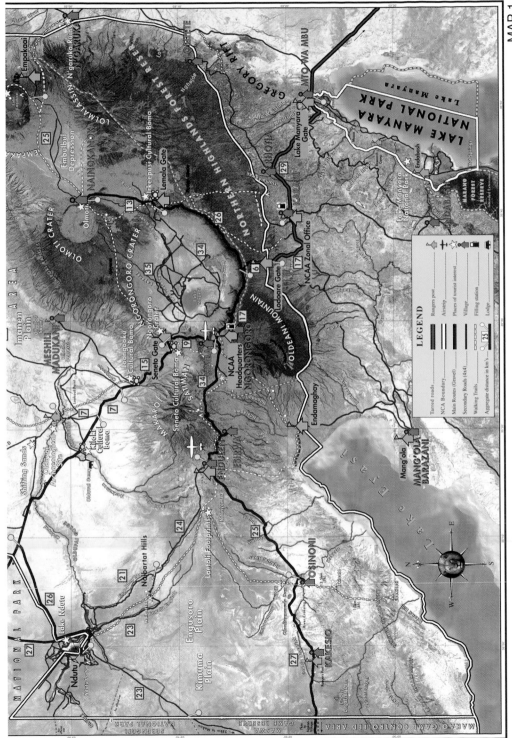

MAP 1

(vi)

MAP OF TANZANIA

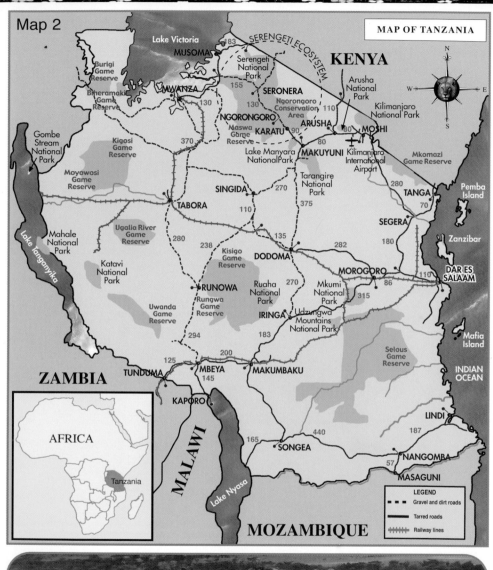

Map 2

MAP OF TANZANIA

Lake Victoria
MUSOMA
83
SERENGETI ECOSYSTEM
KENYA

Burigi Game Reserve
Serengeti National Park
155
SERONERA
Arusha National Park

MWANZA
130
NGORONGORO
Ngorongoro Conservation Area
130
110
Kilimanjaro National Park

Biheramaki Game Reserve
370
KARATU
90
ARUSHA
80
MOSHI

Gombe Stream National Park
Kigosi Game Reserve
Maswa Game Reserve
Lake Manyara NationalPark
MAKUYUNI
Kilimanjaro International Airport
Mkomazi Game Reserve

Moyowosi Game Reserve
SINGIDA
270
Tarangire National Park
280
TANGA
Pemba Island

Lake Tanganyika
Mahale National Park
TABORA
110
375
SEGERA
70

Ugalia River Game Reserve
280
135
282
180
Zanzibar

Katavi National Park
238
Kisigo Game Reserve
DODOMA
MOROGORO
DAR ES SALAAM

RUNOWA
Ruaha National Park
270
Mkumi National Park
86
110

Uwanda Game Reserve
Rungwa Game Reserve
IRINGA
Udzungwa Mountains National Park
315
Mafia Island

294
183
Selous Game Reserve
INDIAN OCEAN

ZAMBIA
125
200
TUNDUMA
MBEYA
MAKUMBAKU

145
KAPORO
LINDI

AFRICA
Tanzania
MALAWI
165
SONGEA
440
187

NANGOMBA
57
MASAGUNI

Lake Nyasa
MOZAMBIQUE

LEGEND
- - - - Gravel and dirt roads
――――― Tarred roads
++++++ Railway lines

A typical scene in Tanzania - Maasai herdsmen with cattle

INTRODUCTION

Lions in the Ngorongoro Crater

INTRODUCTION

The Ngorongoro Conservation Area (NCA) is quite simply the most spectacular tourist destination in Africa - unequalled in its magnificence, its scenic beauty, its wildlife and its atmosphere. The ever-changing weather patterns provide a dramatic backdrop to the scenery and wildlife, creating clouds which pour in over the highlands like giant waves.

The Ngorongoro Highlands inspires one to want to learn more about the geology of the area. It is almost as if each mountain, crater, caldera and gorge takes on a persona of its own, telling the story of an era when violent earth movements and eruptions continually changed the landscape, creating clouds of volcanic ash and earth-trembling rumbles.

This was also a time when our own ancient ancestors walked the earth, first living as vegetarians and later, hunting animals by means of stone tools. Layer upon layer of volcanic ash preserved the fossil evidence, providing us with the opportunity to read the 'archaeological diary' within the layers of the Olduvai Gorge, the famous archaeological site situated inside the NCA.

There are nine craters in the NCA but by far the most impressive is the Ngorongoro Crater, which forms a haven within a haven of protected areas, attracting a truly staggering number and variety of wildlife. During the rainy season the animal numbers in the NCA are multiplied many times over as the Wildebeest, Zebra and other migratory species descend upon the Short Grass Plains.

Added to the beautiful scenery, the archaeological wealth and the wildlife, is a proud people - the Maasai - a pastoral tribe which has managed to preserve its culture over hundreds of years, living in total harmony with the wild animals.

All the above makes for a unique and unforgettable wildlife experience.

A trip of a lifetime!

Clouds pouring over the Ngorongoro Crater

MAP 3

Map of Africa, showing the locality of Tanzania

MAP 4

Map of Tanzania, showing the locality of the NCA

Location The NCA is situated in northern Tanzania and lies between 02°30'S and 03°40'S and 34°50'E and 36°00'E. To the east and south lies the Gregory Rift Valley with Lake Manyara, Lake Eyasi, Lake Natron and the active volcano - Oldoinyo Lengai. On the west it borders Serengeti National Park and in the north lies the Loliondo Game Controlled Area. The NCA is about 170km west of Arusha.

The Serengeti Ecosystem The NCA is safely nestled within game management areas, forming part of the Serengeti Ecosystem which includes the NCA, the Serengeti National Park, the Loliondo Game Controlled Area, the Maswa Game Reserve, the Grumeti Game Reserve, the Ikorongo Game Controlled Area and the Masai Mara Game Reserve, the latter being in Kenya. The ecosystem covers an area of just under 30 000km^2. This ecosystem completely encompasses the traditional migratory routes of the wild ungulates, allowing free movement of game, even across international borders.

INTRODUCTION

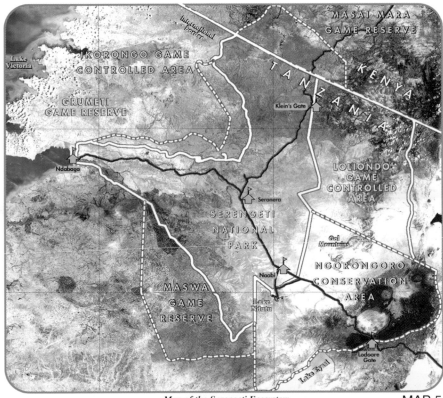

Map of the Serengeti Ecosystem

MAP 5

3

Size and elevation

Size of the NCA   The NCA covers a large conservation area of 8 292km² (3 200 square miles). The Ngorongoro Highlands Forest Reserve is situated within the NCA, on the eastern side, and it covers about 20% thereof.

Size of the Ngorongoro Crater   The Ngorongoro Crater is the sixth largest caldera (collapsed crater) in the world.   The first, second, third and fifth largest ones all occur in Japan and the fourth largest is in the Philippines.   The Ngorongoro Crater, however, has the distinction of being the largest unbroken, unflooded caldera.   It is 2 440m above sea level at its highest point and the floor varies between 1 830m in the north-east to 1 700m at Lake Magadi.   The rim of the crater stands 610m above the floor and the surface area covers ±304km².   It is slightly oval in shape, being 21km along its east-west axis and ±18km along the north-south axis (Pickering, 1993).   The distance from Lemala Gate to the end of the ascent road is 32km and from Seneto Gate to Lemala Gate is 34km.

Elevation   The NCA region varies in altitude between 3 700m above sea level at the highest point, which is at Lolmalasin Crater, to as little as 1 030m at Lake Eyasi.   For the elevation of the other craters, see pg 9.

Establishment of the NCA

In 1959 the Serengeti National Park was divided into the Serengeti National Park (SNP) and the NCA.   All Maasai residents in the SNP were asked to relocate to the NCA. After independence in 1961, a Conservator was appointed to take over the administration of the NCA and henceforth the administration was run by the Ngorongoro Conservation Area Authority (NCAA).   (See pg 15 for more details.)

Climate

There is much variation in climate within the NCA, mainly because of the altitude differences. There is a dry season from June to October and a wet season from November to May. The wet season is divided into the 'short rains' (Nov-Dec) and the 'long rains' (Feb-May). The 'short rains' are brought about by the northern monsoon and the 'long rains' by the south-eastern monsoon. It is often cloudy on the highlands and in summer it rains almost every day.

Rainfall   Annual rainfall varies from 450mm on the plains in the north-west to over 1 600mm on the highlands.   The highest rainfall area is on the eastern and southern sides of the highlands that face into the south-eastern winds. Therefore the vegetation on both sides of the eastern rim is heavily wooded and lush, acting as an important catchment area.   The driest parts are on the western and north-western sides of the highlands which lie in the so-called 'rain-shadow' of the highlands, e.g. Olduvai Gorge, the Serengeti Plains, Sale Plains and Ndutu. It is called the 'rain-shadow' because the clouds come in from the Indian Ocean in the west and are 'broken' by the highlands, resulting in rain.   The clouds that manage to pass the highlands usually evaporate before they can supply rain. The western side of the crater, the side of the Seneto descent road, is visibly drier if one looks at the vegetation, especially the lack of trees. The vegetation consists mainly of grasses, small shrubs and succulents that have adapted to the dry conditions, most visibly the Candelabra Tree (*Euphorbia spp.*).

Climate continued

It is common to have dark clouds and heavy rain on the rim whilst the crater floor enjoys bright sunshine. Interestingly, there is even a variation in rainfall on the crater floor itself with only 300-380mm in the western and central areas and 510-760mm on the eastern side.

Temperature Temperatures in the NCA vary from 3°C to 35°C. Frost occurs on the highest mountain tops and temperatures are always lower along the rim of the Ngorongoro Crater than on its floor. It can become freezing cold in summer when it rains, especially when the wind blows. The coldest months are from June to August. Log fires are essential in winter, lending a cosy atmosphere to the lodges on the crater rim, all of which have huge fireplaces.

Ngorongoro Crater during the rainy season

Ngorongoro Crater during the dry season

Road system of the NCA

The ±160km road from Arusha to the NCA's Lodoare Gate is now tarred. All the roads within the NCA are not tarred. The main roads from Lodoare Gate to Naabi Gate, the rim road of the Ngorongoro Crater and the road from Ngorongoro - Endulen - Kakesio are all gravelled. The main roads within the Ngorongoro Crater are also gravelled. All other roads in the NCA are secondary game drive roads. A 4x4 vehicle is essential. The distances between the main tourist areas are as indicated below. Refer to the map on pg (v).

NCAA Headquarters	-	Lodoare Gate	19km	NCAA Headquarters	-	Lake Ndutu (via Olduvai)....90km
NCAA Headquarters	-	Lemala Gate (along rim)	39km	NCAA Headquarters	-	Lake Ndutu (via Endulen)...84km
NCAA Headquarters	-	Olmoti Crater	52km	NCAA Headquarters	-	Naabi Gate....83km
NCAA Headquarters	-	Empakaai Crater	81km	Olduvai Museum	-	Olkarien Gorge....60km
NCAA Headquarters	-	Seneto Entrance Gate	9km	Olduvai Museum	-	Nasera Rock....55km
NCAA Headquarters	-	Olduvai Gorge	42km	Olduvai Museum	-	Naabi Gate....54km
NCAA Headquarters	-	Olkarien Gorge	86km	Seneto Gate	-	Lemala Gate....35km
NCAA Headquarters	-	Nasera Rock	96km	Lodoare Gate	-	Naabi Gate....101km

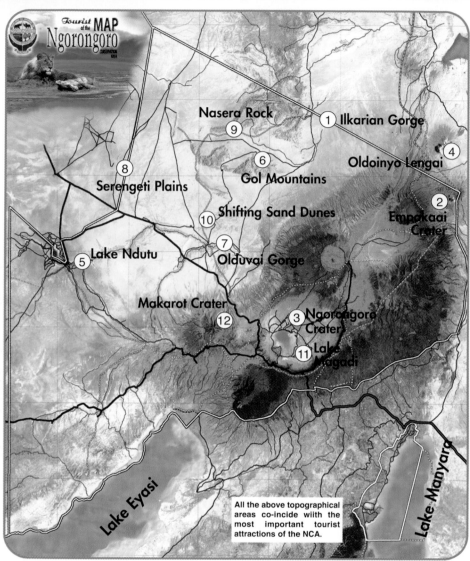

Topography of the Ngorongoro Conservation Area

MAP 6

All the above topographical areas co-incide with the most important tourist attractions of the NCA.

①	Ilkarian Gorge		⑦	Olduvai Gorge
②	Empakaai Crater		⑧	Serengeti Plains
③	Ngorongoro Crater		⑨	Nasera Rock
④	Oldoinyo Lengai		⑩	Shifting Sand Dunes
⑤	Lake Ndutu		⑪	Lake Magadi
⑥	Gol Mountains		⑫	Makarot Crater

INTRODUCTION

① *Ilkarian Gorge*

② *Empakaai Crater*

③ *Ngorongoro Crater*

④ *Oldoinyo Lengai*

⑤ *Lake Ndutu*

⑥ *Gol Mountains*

⑦ *Olduvai Gorge*

⑧ *Serengeti Plains*

INTRODUCTION

⑨ *Nasera Rock*

⑩ *Shifting Sand Dunes*

⑪ *Lake Magadi*

⑫ *Makarot Crater (mountain in the background)*

The main topographical features of the NCA

This section on topography has been included to familiarise the reader with the names and locations of the main topographical features of the NCA. The formation of these features is described in more detail in the section on Geology, pg 69.

Meanings of Names

'Oldoinyo'	-	'Mountain'
'Engeju'	-	'River'
'Ang'ata'	-	'Plain'
'Losirua'	-	'Eland Mountain'
'Oldoinyo Lengai'	-	'Mountain of God'
'Soit'	-	'Rock'
'Magadi'	-	'Soda' or 'Salt'
'Lerai'	-	'Fever Tree'

Gol Mountains   The Gol Mountains are situated in the north-west of the NCA. These mountains are some of the oldest geological formations in the area, formed more than 500 million years ago. The highlands were formed ±15 million years ago and the Ngorongoro Crater took on its present form only two to three million years ago.   In geological terms, at least, that is fairly recent! The Gol Mountains rise about 915m above the Ang'ata Sale Plains. Lololo is the highest peak of the Gol Mountains at 2 350m above sea level.   The most interesting features of the Gol Mountains are Ilkarian Gorge and Nasera Rock.   Ilkarian Gorge is a major nesting site of the Ruppell's Griffon (a vulture) and Nasera Rock is a granite monolith which rises nearly 100m above the plains.

The Ngorongoro Highlands   The eastern part of the NCA consists of the Ngorongoro Highlands - an area comprising mountains, craters, calderas, valleys and depressions. The highlands were formed by volcanic activity - cones building up around vents in the earth's crust, followed by expansion, merging and the collapse of the cones.

INTRODUCTION

The vegetation on the eastern side of the highlands is much more lush than on the western side because the clouds come in from the Indian Ocean in the east and 'break' against the highlands. About 20% (893km^2) of the NCA consists of the Ngorongoro Highlands Forest Reserve - a pristine rain forest covering the eastern side of the highlands. The Ngorongoro Highlands is an important catchment area for the lowlands. Rainwater is absorbed by the porous volcanic soils and reappears as springs below, flowing into the basins within the Rift Valley such as Lake Eyasi, Lake Manyara, Olmkoko and Lake Natron.

The Craters and Calderas There are nine craters within the boundaries of the NCA and one on the north-eastern corner (Kerimasi Crater). The names of the craters from east to west are Keramasi, Empakaai, Lolmalasin, Losirua, Olmoti, Ngorongoro, Oldeani, Loroklukunya, Sadiman and Makarot. The highest crater is Lolmalasin at 3 700m above sea level. According to Pickering, 1993, the following are the highest points of some of the craters:

Lolmalasin	-	3 700m
Losirua	-	3 260m
Empakaai	-	3 220m
Oldeani	-	3 180m
Makarot	-	3 130m
Olmoti	-	3 080m
Sadiman	-	2 860m
Ngorongoro	-	2 440m
Kerimasi	-	2 300m

Before it collapsed, the Ngorongoro Crater was said to have been 4 587m above sea level. Kilimanjaro, which is a crater, not a caldera, is the highest mountain in Africa at 5 895m.

Just outside the northern boundary is the famous active volcano, Oldoinyo Lengai, which rises 1 830m above the valley floor.

A bit to the north-east is the extinct volcano Mosonik. Some of the craters, such as Ngorongoro, Empakaai and Olmoti, are not true craters but are actually calderas. A caldera is formed when a circular fault in the wall of the volcano causes it to collapse into itself to form a crater floor.

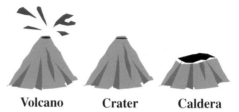

Volcano   Crater   Caldera

Different stages of volcanoes

The Short Grass Plains The Short Grass Plains cover most of the north-western part of the NCA and consist of the Serengeti Plains which stretches up to Lake Ndutu, the Ang'ata Kiti Plain and the Ang'ata Sale Plain (see map on pg (v)). It covers about half of the entire NCA and falls in the 'rain shadow' of the highlands, making it much drier than the highlands. The plains were formed by layers of volcanic ash emitted by the volcanoes of the highlands. Volcanic soils are high in nutrients, supporting a healthy grass cover that can sustain thousands of ungulates. The Sale Plain is at an altitude of 1 280m near the eastern side of the Gol Mountains, gently sloping to 1 230m near Mosonik. The Serengeti Plain is 1 920m at its highest point, gently sloping southward to the Olduvai Gorge which stands at 1 600m.

The Salt Lakes Lake Masek is within the boundaries of the NCA, but Lake Ndutu falls within the Serengeti National Park. There is also a lake within the Ngorongoro Crater, Lake Magadi. 'Magadi' is the Swahili name and 'Makat', the Maasai name, both meaning 'soda' or 'salt'. Lake Empakaai partly covers the floor of Empakaai Crater and is a salt lake. Unlike most other salt lakes, which are shallow, Lake Empakaai is about 60m deep.

INTRODUCTION

The Basins Basins are low-lying areas that receive water from the surrounding catchment areas. The basins within the NCA are Lake Magadi in the Ngorongoro Crater, Lake Empakaai in the Empakaai Crater, Olbalbal Depression, Embulbul Depression and Malanja Depression. The Olbalbal Depression lies to the east of the Ngorongoro Crater. It is ±1 370m above sea level. Embulbul lies between Olmoti, Losirua, Lolmalasin and Empakaai Craters. The floor of Embulbul stands at 2 320m. Malanja Depression lies south-west of the Ngorongoro Crater and its southern boundary is formed by Loroklukunya and Sadiman Craters. The Malanja Depression lies at 2 100m above sea level.

Rivers The Munge River originates in the Olmoti Crater, providing fresh water to the Mandusi Swamp within the Ngorongoro Crater. The Lonyonyokie River originates on Oldeani Mountain and provides fresh water to the Gorigor Swamp. The Olduvai River runs along the Olduvai Gorge but it is dry for most of the year. The Ilkarian River carved a deep gorge - Ilkarian Gorge - through the Gol Mountains, but also remains dry for most of the year.

Olduvai Gorge The famous Olduvai Gorge runs through the Short Grass Plains. Faulting caused the land to tilt towards the Olbalbal Depression (to the east of Olduvai). Thus, the waters from Lake Ndutu and Lake Masek cut a gorge through the plains - the Olduvai Gorge - which empties into the Olbalbal Depression.

Swamps In the Ngorongoro Crater there are two swamps, the Mandusi Swamp that is fed by the Olmoti Crater via the Munge River and the Gorigor Swamp that is fed by the Lonyonyokie River, which originates on Mount Oldeani. To the west of the Ngorongoro Crater is the Olbalbal Swamp, fed by the Olduvai River, all the way from Lake Ndutu and Lake Masek.

Springs Inside the Ngorongoro Crater there are two springs fed by underground streams from the surrounding highlands - Ngoitokitok Spring in the east and Seneto Spring in the south-west.

Ilkarian Gorge

INTRODUCTION

Tribes of the area

Maasai women

NCAA

HISTORY AND PEOPLE

The following is a chronological description of the people that inhabited the area over the last 10 000 years and before.

MORE THAN 10 000 YEARS AGO

Hadzabe or Watindiga tribe   The earliest known human inhabitants of the area were probably of the Hadzabe or Watindiga tribe whom today live near Lake Eyasi. They were not a warrior tribe but lived as hunter-gatherers and hunted by means of bows and poisoned arrows.   They have a distinctive appearance with prominent high cheekbones, a slight build and light skin.   Today, they smoke bone or metal pipes and speak a click language much like their ancestors did.   Interestingly, all the above characteristics correspond with that of the San (also known as Bushmen) of Botswana, Namibia, Angola and South Africa, ±5 000km to the south.

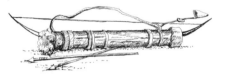

±10 000 YEARS AGO

The Stone-bowl people   There is bone evidence of the presence of cattle which dates back about 10 000 years.   This was probably when the first pastoralists moved into the area. These people are generally referred to as the Stone-bowl people because of the evidence of stone bowls that were used for grinding plant material.   In these sites there is also evidence of pottery, other stone tools, beads, bits of iron, ochre and communal graves that were covered in stone. The Stone-bowl people disappeared about one thousand years ago.

±2 000 YEARS AGO

The Iraqw   The next tribe to inhabit the area was the Iraqw, probably of Ethiopian origin, judging by the Cushitic language they speak. They arrived about 2 000 years or more ago.   Today they live on the eastern side of the Ngorongoro Highlands towards Lake Manyara.

500–400 YEARS AGO

The Bantu-speaking tribes   The Bantu-speaking tribes occur mainly in southern Africa, yet there are over 100 tribes in Tanzania.   They arrived 400-500 years ago and settled in the coastal regions and at the lakes. The Sonjo is one tribe that settled in the Ngorongoro area and today they live in the vicinity of Lake Natron.

Engaruka ruins   At the foot of Empakaai Crater, just outside the NCA, are the ruins of an old city, Engaruka, which dates back about 500 years.   It consists of terraces built into the mountain with the remains of stone houses and an ancient irrigation system. It is not clear which tribe built this city.

±300 YEARS AGO

The Datoga   The Iraqw were probably forced out by a warrior pastoralist tribe, the Datoga, also known as the Barbaig or Mang'ati.   They moved in about 300 years ago and today can be found in the Lake Eyasi area.

±200 YEARS AGO

The Maasai   About 200 years ago the Maasai moved into the Serengeti/Ngorongoro area, probably in search of grazing for their cattle.   Being the fierce warrior tribe they are, many battles over the area followed, mainly with the Datoga.   The Maasai eventually secured the area but even today they speak of their ancient enemy with deference, referring to the Datoga as the Mang'ati, which means 'respected enemy'.   (See box on opposite page for more details.)

Maasai warrior

THE MAASAI

It is generally believed that the Maasai tribe is a mixture of Nilotes (people from the Nile area) and Hamites (people from North Africa). Most Maasai tribes cover their bodies with ochre, a yellow pigment derived from iron-rich soils which they mix with animal fat. Interestingly, their togas, sandals and short stabbing swords worn in sheaths on their belts, show a remarkable resemblance to the ancient Romans who once occupied north Africa. It is thought that they migrated along the Nile into the Lake Turkana area of Kenya in about the 15th century. 'Maasai' means 'speaker of the Maa language', but there are several Maa dialects. Linguistically, the Maasai are closely related to the Bari of Sudan.

Maasai cattle

The cattle of the Maasai are not as productive as other domestic stock but they are hardy and disease resistant. During the rains, when the wildebeests come to the Short Grass Plains, many Maasai do take the precaution of moving their herds into the mountains to prevent them from contracting malignant catarrh fever, a contagious disease carried by Wildebeests. Their cattle are almost sacred to the Maasai and are only slaughtered on very special occasions. They are used for exchange and to legalise marriages. Cattle are very important for the milk that they yield - the staple diet of the Maasai. They drink it fresh or make a yogurt-like sour drink from it which they carry in gourds. Where possible, they include grain in their diet.

Their houses are constructed of wood, covered with mud. The soil is often mixed with cattle droppings and urine to make it waterproof. The houses are built in a circle and the cattle and goats are kept in the inner circle at night to protect them from predators (Martin, 1993).

From 1890 to 1900, the Maasai were severely affected by Rinderpest, drought, famine and locusts. Their biggest setback, however, was probably colonisation by the Europeans. For centuries the natural forces such as seasonal cycles, droughts and the Tsetse Fly protected the Serengeti by forcing the pastoralists to practice a form of rotational grazing, allowing the grass a period of recovery. Since grazing was not restricted, it was quite possible to do that.

Typical Maasai village with huts made from mud and wood

The Tsetse Fly is included as 'protector' since fear of the disease forced the pastoralists to avoid Tsetse Fly ridden areas. The Tsetse Fly carries a virus that causes ndigana in cattle and sleeping sickness in humans, the effects of which may lead to death. The effects in humans and animals are the same - it affects the brain, causing extreme drowsiness. The technical term for this disease is *encephalitis lethargica*.

With colonisation things changed rapidly for the Maasai, especially when farmers and hunters moved into the area. Legislation under colonial rule denied the Maasai much of their previous dry season grazing. In 1958, 12 elders signed a treaty in which they relinquished their rights to graze their cattle in the Serengeti National Park. About 1 000 Maasai, 25 000 cattle and 15 000 goats and sheep, were translocated to the NCA. Today about 60 000 Maasai live within the boundaries of the NCA. It is estimated that there were about 300 000 to 400 000 Maasai living in northern Tanzania in 1993 (Martin, 1993).

Maasai children

Young Maasai boys during initiation

Maasai men

Maasai women

LATE 1800s

German colonialisation During the end of the 19th century, the Germans occupied Tanzania and called it Deutch Ost-Afrika. By the turn of the century, hunters and explorers were well acquainted with the area.

EARLY 1900s

Hunting and farming The early 1900s experienced a hunting boom. Recreational, trophy and ivory hunting took its toll and it soon became obvious that the area needed protection. Farmers also moved in. Two German brothers, named Siebentopf, divided the Ngorongoro Crater floor and claimed it for their exclusive use. The remains of the buildings can still be seen today, one near the Rangers Post in the south-west and one to the north-east, just north of the Munge Stream, on a small hill. The Germans realised that some legislation was necessary to control hunting and farming and they made several attempts to put this in place. However, World War I came along and priorities changed.

Hunting was rife during the early 1900s

1911 – 1913

Early scientists In 1911, a certain Professor Wilhelm Kattwinkel, a German naturalist, stumbled upon some fossils whilst collecting butterflies in the Olduvai Gorge. His report was followed up in 1913 by an expedition led by Professor Hans Reck, a German palaeontologist.

1921 – 1929

Establishment of the Serengeti Game Reserve After World War I the British took over the area and most Germans left. They called it 'Tanganyika Territory'. Today, Tanzania is a united republic between Tanganyika (the mainland) and Zanzibar (the isles of Pemba and Linguja). In 1921 the Game Conservation Ordinance was introduced by the British, and in 1928 hunting and agriculture were prohibited in the Ngorongoro Crater. In 1929 a 2 286km^2 area in the central part of the Serengeti - Seronera area - was declared a game reserve, but sport hunting was still allowed.

±1930s

Developing the area Development started around the 1930s. During this time a road was constructed from Karatu to Loliondo, the latter being the administrative centre of the area. A road was built from the Ngorongoro Crater to Mwanza, a village on the banks of Lake Victoria.

Leakey expedition In 1931 an expedition organised by Louis Leakey with Profressor Hans Reck was undertaken to the Olduvai Area to search for fossils. In 1935 lion hunting was banned in the Seronera Valley.

±1940s

Start of tourism The start of tourism was marked by the building of a log cabin lodge on the rim of the crater around this time.

1951

Establishment of the Serengeti National Park In 1951 the Serengeti National Park was finally established. At that time, it included the Ngorongoro Conservation Area (NCA) and there were still Maasai living in the Serengeti.

1958 – 1959

Establishment of the NCA In 1958 a document was signed by 12 Maasai elders, where they agreed to relocate to the NCA. In 1959 the Serengeti National Park was divided into the Serengeti National Park (SNP) and the NCA.

HISTORY AND PEOPLE

1961

NCAA After independence in 1961, a Conservator was appointed to take over the administration of the NCA and henceforth the administration was run by the Ngorongoro Conservation Area Authority (NCAA).

1979 – 1981

World Heritage Site and International Biosphere Reserve In 1979 the NCA was declared a World Heritage Site. In 1981 the NCA and the Serengeti National Park were declared an International Biosphere Reserve.

BERNHARD AND MICHAEL GRZIMEK_

During the early 1950s, Professor Bernhard Grzimek and his son Michael flew from Germany in a small aircraft to do a count of the migrating herds of the Serengeti. Professor Grzimek was the Director of the Frankfurt Zoo and President of the Frankfurt Zoological Society (FZS) at the time. Thus started a long and fruitful relationship between the FZS and Tanzania.

The Bernhard and Michael Grzimek Memorial Stone marks their graves

They produced the famous book and film 'Serengeti Shall not Die', which was translated into all the major languages and the proceeds of which were ploughed back into conservation in Tanzania. Sadly, Michael died in 1959 in an aeroplane crash in the Ngorongoro Crater during one of these counts. His grave can be seen on the rim of the crater. His father devoted much of the rest of his life to conservation in Tanzania and died of natural causes in 1987. He was buried next to his son on the rim of the Ngorongoro Crater.

MICHAEL GRZIMEK
12. 4. 1934 — 10. 1. 1959
HE GAVE ALL HE POSSESSED
INCLUDING HIS LIFE
FOR THE WILD ANIMALS OF AFRICA

PROFESSOR BERNHARD GRZIMEK
1909 - 1987

A LIFETIME OF CARING
FOR WILD ANIMALS
AND THEIR PLACE ON OUR PLANET
IT IS BETTER TO LIGHT A CANDLE
THAN TO CURSE THE DARKNESS

Close-up of the Memorial Stone

In late December of 1957, Professor Bernhard Grzimek of the Frankfurt Zoological Society and his son Michael flew a small plane from Germany to Tanganyika to conduct the first aerial surveys of game in the Serengeti National Park. Thus began one of the great conservation efforts of this century. Operating with limited supplies, in remote and inaccessible areas, they succeeded in providing the Tanganyikan government with the first systematically collected data on the abundance and distribution of the Serengeti's many game animals. Through their pioneering scientific work, and the popularity of the resulting book and film "Serengeti Shall Not Die", they revealed the grandeur of the Serengeti to the world, and awakened a world-wide desire to preserve this magnificent ecosystem.

Bernard and Michael Grzimek.
This photograph forms part of the exhibit at the Seronera Information Centre

Gol Mountains area

Bookings

If you plan to stay in a hotel, bookings can be done directly. Contact details of companies are provided on pg 173. If you are planning to camp inside the NCA, it is not essential to book in advance but bookings can be made via any of the following contacts:

Contact details
Tel: (+255) (27) 250-3339 / 254-4625
Fax: (+255) (27) 254-8752
Email: ncaa_faru@cybernet.co.tz /
ncaa_info@cybernet.co.tz
ncaa info@africaonline.co.tz
Website: www.ngorongoro-crater-africa.org

How to get there

BY AIR

One needs to fly to Kilimanjaro International Airport at Moshi, situated at the foot of Mount Kilimanjaro. From there one can get a charter flight, take a taxi or make use of the free shuttle service. The distance from Moshi to Arusha is about 55km (see pg 173 for contact details of airline companies).

BY ROAD

Take note: The road from Arusha to Lodoare Entrance Gate is 160km long. As of recently, the entire journey is on tarmac and it takes about two hours. Unless you stay on the main roads, which are gravelled, a 4x4 vehicle is essential when entering the Ngorongoro Conservation Area and the Serengeti National Park.

Starting at Arusha For most people the journey will start at Arusha, which is situated in northern Tanzania about midway between the Cape (southern point of South Africa) and Cairo. Arusha was given city status in July 2005. It is situated at the foot of Mount Meru and is surrounded by coffee and banana plantations. It is about 160km east of the NCA and 290km from the Serengeti Entrance Gate at Naabi.

Where to stay in Arusha There are many options to choose from, but based on my personal experience, I can recommend the following: If you want to stay in luxury but still be close to town, I suggest Kibo Palace or the Impala Hotel. If you prefer luxury but

want to be outside town, the best choices are Ngurduto Mountain Lodge or Arumeru River Lodge, both of which are situated at Usa-River near the entrance of Arusha National Park. If you want a cheaper option but still enjoy absolute comfort, I recommend the Le Jacaranda Hotel, which is situated close to town. I always stay there and can guarantee a warm, friendly welcome – very good value for money. They have a restaurant and breakfast is included. If you are camping or want a cheap room for the night, Masai Camp is the best place. Their prices are extremely reasonable and they have a bar and restaurant. At Masai Camp they offer safaris through Tropical Trails. So, if you do not have a 4x4, you can leave your vehicle at the camp and join a safari from there. Contact details of all the above lodges are on pg 173.

Arusha to Makuyuni From the clock-tower in the centre of Arusha one travels west for ±83km to Makuyuni, which is marked by a few shops and curio sellers. If you continue south along this road it will take you to Tarangire National Park. If you turn right (west) at Makuyuni, onto a tarred road, it will take you to the NCA and the Serengeti. This road is tarred up to Lodoare Entrance Gate.

Makuyuni to Mto-wa-Mbu About 36km after Makuyuni one reaches the small village of Mto-wa-Mbu, which means 'mosquito creek' in Swahili. It is a delightful, lush village, nestled under huge, shady trees with a number of fruit and curio stalls - a welcome oasis after a long drive and the ideal place to stock up with fruit and vegtables.

There is ample accommodation and camping available in and around the village at different price levels. If you want to stay in style, opt for one of the lodges on the escarpment - all of which offer incredible views of the Rift Valley. The entrance to Lake Manyara National Park is inside the town, and a visit is highly recommended.

The Gregory Rift Escarp to Karatu
Almost directly after leaving Mto-wa-Mbu, one ascends a steep escarpment (about 600m) which offers a magnificent view of Lake Manyara and the Gregory Rift Valley. It is worth stopping at the summit to enjoy the view and to take photographs. There are also toilet facilities. The road passes through the Mbulu farmlands where wheat, coffee and maize are grown. The distance from Mto-wa-Mbu to Karatu is ±27km.

Karatu Karatu is your last chance to buy some provisions and fill up with fuel, which is cheaper here than inside the NCA. There are banks where one can change foreign currency. The market in Karatu is excellent and worth a visit. Karatu is only 17km from Lodoare Entrance Gate. It is the ideal place to stay over and do day visits to the NCA. I always stay at Kudu Lodge which offers chalets, a bar, restaurant as well as camping, the latter at only about US$10 per person. They have a good restaurant too. They offer safaris from Kudu Lodge with Macho Ya Tanzania, the safari company that is based there. There is also a luxury lodge about 5km before you reach Lodoare Gate from Karatu, on the left hand side. It is called Ngorongoro Farm House and the entrance is indicated along the tarred road. Bookings can be done through Kibo Safaris. Contact details for all the above lodges are provided on pg 173 / 174.

Another great thing about Karatu, is that one can do walking trails from there to the Ngorongoro Highlands Forest Reserve. These are some of the most spectacular walks in the Ngorongoro. Just report to the NCAA Zonal Office and they will supply you with a guide. Most of these are day walks and one can see waterfalls as well as excavations, resembling caves, made by elephants in the mineral rich soils of the highlands (see pg 23 for details on walking trails).

Lodoare Entrance Gate After a drive of ±160km from Arusha, one reaches the Lodoare Entrance Gate to the NCA. At the gate one needs to pay daily entrance fees. Keep in mind that if you are in transit to the Serengeti, you still have to pay the daily fees but it is well worth it! Try to be at the gate early in the morning to make the best of your day - it opens at 6h00. There is a small information centre at the gate where books and maps are for sale.

The Rim of the Ngorongoro Crater After leaving Lodoare Gate, one ascends to the Ngorongoro Crater wall through magnificent scenery dominated by giant trees. After ±6km you will reach the rim. (See pg 77 for details on the vegetation along this road.) You will know you have reached the rim when the most incredible view of the Ngorongoro Crater opens up in front of you. One can stop at the Bernhard and Michael Grzimek memorial stone and get out of your vehicle to take photographs. It offers one of the best views of the Ngorongoro Crater. Further along this road you will see another stone marker which marks the actual graves of the Grzimeks (see pg 16 for deatils on the Grzimeks).

View of Lake Manyara and the Gregory Rift Valley from the escarpment

TOURIST INFORMATION

Announce your arrival ±14km after the view-point, their is a well marked turn-off to the left which leads to the Tourist Office and the NCAA Headquarters. Here you have to announce your arrival. Take note, if you wish to go down the Crater, you need to be accompanied by a guide from the tourist office and there is an additional service fee to be payed of ±US$100 per vehicle per day. One can also pay camping fees here. The tourist office will direct you to the camping site.

Fuel The filling station is next to the NCAA headquarters.

Places to stay

CAMPING

No one is allowed to spend the night inside the Ngorongoro Crater. There is only one public camp site - Simba A - situated ±3km west of the turn-off to the tourist office on the rim of the crater. It is well marked and close to the main road. There are toilets, showers and hot water. Keep in mind, it becomes icy cold up there. It is advisable to take some wood along since it is prohibited to collect firewood inside the NCA. One is allowed to make fires at designated sites but camp fires should be extinguished after use to prevent the spread of veld fires. A gas burner is ideal for cooking. One can also join a safari company in which case you can stay in the special camp sites. Contact details for safari companies are provided on pg 174.

A mobile safari camp belonging to Unique Safaris

Simba A Camp Site

LUXURY LODGES

There are four luxury lodges to choose from, all situated on the Ngorongoro Crater wall. They are Ngorongoro Wildlife Lodge, Ngorongoro Serena Lodge, Ngorongoro Crater Lodge and Ngorongoro Sopa Lodge. The first three are situated on the southern rim but Ngorongoro Sopa Lodge is situated on the northern rim near Lemala Gate. It is impossible to recommend one in favour the other as they are all exquisite, each one of them offering breathtaking views of the crater, high quality service, swimming pools, bar, restaurant and fireplaces for those cold,

Ngorogoro Crater Logde

rainy days. Many of the lodges offer reasonable discounts during the off season (January to April). Contact details for all the above lodges can be obtained on pg 173.

Places to stay continued

NCAA

Ngorogoro Serena Logde

Ngorongoro Wildlife Lodge

Ngorongoro Sopa Lodge

Best season to visit

Rainy season (November to April) The short rains are from November to December and the long rains from February to April, the latter generally being considered the off season. However, the rainy season is a very exciting time of year as this is when the animals congregate on the Short Grass Plains to have their young. Late February, early March is usually a good time to see the migration on the plains. In turn, this attracts large numbers of predators and results in spectacular interactions between predators and prey. Keep in mind that part of the Serengeti Plains fall within the NCA. Birds abound at this time and the wild flowers are in bloom, streaking the landscape with white, yellow and purple and attracting a menagerie of butterflies. The rainstorms are dramatic and usually short-lived, but the cloud formations and the build-up of rainstorms is a sight to behold. On the downside, you may get stuck a few times

and it may rain. In my view, that is a small price to pay for the quality of game-viewing and the scenery. The Short Grass Plains, Ngorongoro and Ndutu are particularly good this time of year. After heavy rains it is not advisable to visit Empakaai Crater as the roads become quite treacherous.

Dry season (May to October) The dry season holds its own beauty. It is generally accepted in other parts of Africa that the dry season is the best time for game viewing because the animals are concentrated along permanent water sources. This is true within the crater where game-viewing is excellent this time of year. However, keep in that the Short Grass Plains become completely devoid of game during this season. This is the best time of year to visit Empakaai and Ndutu also has resident game that remains around the lake all year round.

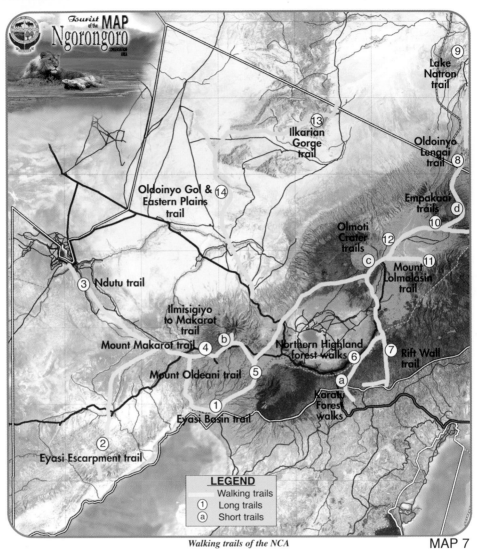

Walking trails of the NCA

MAP 7

Long trails

1. Eyasi Basin trail
2. Eyasi Escarpment trail
3. Ndutu area trail
4. Mount Makarot trail
5. Mount Oldeani trail
6. Northern Highlands forest walks
7. Rift Wall trail
8. Oldoinyo Lengai trail
9. Lake Natron trail
10. Empakaai Crater trail
11. Mount Lolmalasin trail
12. Olmoti Crater trail
13. Ilkarian Gorge trail
14. Oldoinyo Gol and the Eastern Plains trail

Short trails

a. Forest walks from Karatu to waterfalls via Elephant Caves
b. Ilmisigiyo to Makarot summit
c. Olmoti Crater trail
d. Empakaai Crater trail

TOURIST INFORMATION

Walking trails

Take note: The trails are indicated in more detail on the Ngorongoro Tourist Map (A1 size) which is obtainable at the NCAA tourist office, at the gates and in bookshops in Arusha.

Where to book   Long trails should be booked at least 30 days in advance and short trails at least one day ahead of time. Bookings can be done at:
Tel: (+255) (27) 250-3339 / 250-254-4625 / 253-7008 / 253-1019
Fax: (+255) (27) 254-8752
E-mail ncaa_faru@cybernet.co.tz
or ncaa_info@africaonline.co.tz
Website: www.ngorongoro-crater-africa.org

Short trails   The shorter trails, where camping is not involved, can be booked at the NCAA headquarters in Ngorongoro Crater at least one day before departure. The forest walks from Karatu can be organized at the NCAA Zonal Office in Karatu town. They will provide the guides. The Karatu Forest Walk (marked (a) on the map on pg 22) is highly recommended. It follows a route through pristine forest where one can see waterfalls as well as 'elephant caves'. The latter are huge excavations made by elephants. They actually ingest the mineral rich soils to supplement their diet with the necessary minerals to ensure strong bone and teeth formation.

Long trails   The longer walking trails where camping is involved, should be booked at least 30 days in advance to arrange for camping equipment, guides and donkeys to carry the equipment.

Donkeys are used for carrying equipment

Excavations made by Elephants in the mineral-rich soils

Armed guides are provided for your safety against the wild

Waterfall on the Karata Forest Walk

TOURIST INFORMATION

23

TOURIST INFORMATION

WHAT TO TAKE

Camping equipment You have to provide all your own camping equipment and supplies. This includes tents, sleeping bags, food and water. Tents are essential because of the danger of wild animals, which are most active at night.

Gas burners Keep in mind that fires are only allowed at designated sites in the NCA. A small, light-weight gas burner is the best option.

Clothing Take cool and warm clothes as the weather can change instantly. Always carry a rainproof garment. Temperatures can vary from 35° C in the shade to under freezing point in the highlands.

Sun protection Sunblock, sunglasses and a hat are essential.

Water Keep in mind there is virtually no surface water, except in the highlands. The water in the pans are too salty for human consumption. Drink at least five litres of water per day to prevent dehydration. Maasai helpers can be hired and they provide donkeys to carry heavy equipment and water.

Food Work out a day-by-day menu to ensure that you do not carry food that you will not use.

Refuge bags Remember that you are not allowed to bury litter. All refuge must be brought out with you, therefore take refuge bags.

Spade It is essential to take a small spade for digging holes to bury human faeces.

Insect repellent Make sure you take insect repellent, especially for mosquitoes which are not only a nuisance, but can cause malaria.

Binoculars and camera Do not take heavy camera equipment with you. Binoculars are highly recommended.

Torch or small gas light A torch or gas light is essential to see at night.

Matches or lighter One should never be in the bush without matches in the case of an emergency.

TRAIL REGULATIONS

Use only established camp sites By using established camp sites the environmental impact will be reduced.

Do not contaminate water Camp at least 80m away from natural water sources to prevent it from being contaminated. Never use soap or shampoo in natural water sources. Do not bury human faeces near to water.

Camp fires Camp fires are only allowed at designated sites - take a gas burner for cooking.

Do not litter Take great care to bring all litter out with you. Do not bury litter as the animals dig it out. It is not only unsightly but can also be harmful to the animals.

Stick to the trails Reduce environmental impact by sticking to the trails. Take care not to step on sensitive vegetation.

Bury human faeces Take a small spade along and be sure to bury human faeces and toilet paper at least 40cm deep. Toilet paper can be burned but take care not to start a fire.

PLACES TO SEE

A storm building up at Nasera Rock

FINGERTIP FACTS OF THE NGORONGORO CRATER.

Elevation of rim
• Highest point on eastern rim: 2 388 metres above sea level.
• Highest point on western rim: 2 100 metres above sea level.
Elevation of floor: ±1 800 metres above sea level.
Elevation of banks of Lake Magadi: 1 729 metres above sea level.
Surface area of the Caldera: ±304km².
Diameter along east-west axis: 21km.
Diameter along north-south axis: 18km.

NGORONG

NAIGRO

Engitati Hill

Quarry

13

Seneto Entrance Gate

2100m

Ongorlenito Hills

294km to Oldavai Gorge
76km to Serengeti

Seneto
Cultural Boma

View Point

MALANJA
DEPRESSION

Seneto Springs

Hippo Pool

MANDUSI SWAM

Lake
Magadi

OLOROKLUKONYA

Tatogoa
Ritual
Site

Ngorongoro
Serena Lodge

LERAI
FOREST

KIMBA
VILLAGE

Simba B

Simba A

Ngorongoro
Crater
Lodge

Picnic Site
& toilet

NCAA Head Quarters

Tourism Office

Nyati
Camp
Site

Ngorongoro Wildlife Lodge
Grzimek Memorial Grave

NGORONGORO
VILLAGE

Rhino
Lodge

Grzimek Stone

GORIG

NORTHERN HIGHL

35°28'   35°30'   35°32'

Coke's Hartebeest

Elephant

Zebra

Black Rhino

26

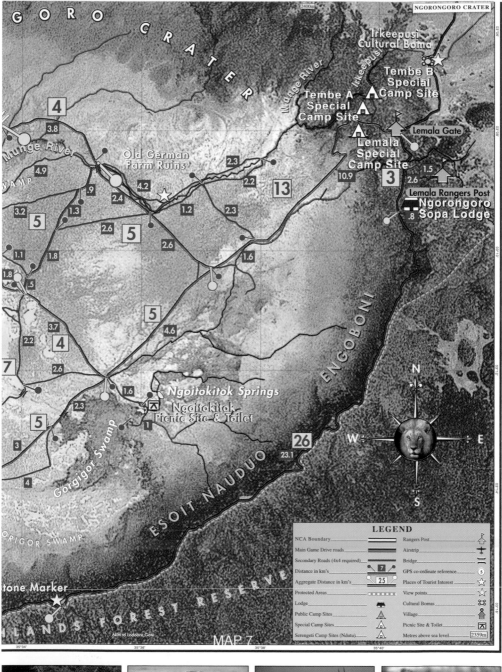

2400m

G O R O   C R A T E R

Munge River

Irkeepusi
Cultural Boma

Tembe B
Special
Camp Site

Tembe A
Special
Camp Site

Lemala Gate

Irkeepusi

Lemala
Special
Camp Site

3

1.5

2.6

Lemala Rangers Post
Ngorongoro
Sopa Lodge

.8

10.9

4

3.8

Munge River

4.9

SWAMP

Old German
Farm Ruins

2.3

2.2

13

.9

2.4

4.2

1.2

2.3

3.2

5

1.3

2.6

5

2.3

1.1

1.8

2.6

1.6

1.8

.5

5

4.6

3.7

4

2.2

ENGOBONI

2.6

7

2.3

1.6

Ngoitokitok Springs
Ngoitokitok
Picnic Site & Toilet

5

3

1

4

Gorgigor Swamp

ESOIT NAUDUO

26

23.1

N

W   E

S

GORIGOR SWAMP

tone Marker

HLANDS   FOREST   RESERVE

6km to Lodoare Gate

MAP 7

35°34'   35°36'   35°38'   35°40'

LEGEND

NCA Boundary	Rangers Post
Main Game Drive roads	Airstrip
Secondary Roads (4x4 required)	Bridge
Distance in km's [7]	GPS co-ordinate reference ⑤
Aggregate Distance in km's [25]	Places of Tourist Interest ☆
Protected Areas	View points ☆
Lodge	Cultural Bomas
Public Camp Sites ▲	Village
Special Camp Sites ▲	Picnic Site & Toilet ⊠
Serengeti Camp Sites (Ndutu) ▲	Metres above sea level 2359m

Leopard

Buffalo

Grants Gazelle

Lion

PLACES TO SEE

The Ngorongoro Crater

Take note: *It is necessary to report at the tourist office first before entering the crater to get a permit and a guide.*

Size and elevation The Ngorongoro Crater is 2 440m above sea level at its highest point on the south-eastern side and the floor varies between 1 830m in the north-east to 1 700m at Lake Magadi. The rim of the crater stands 610m above the floor and the surface area covers ±304km². It is slightly oval in shape, being 21km along its east-west axis and ±18km along the north-south axis (Pickering, 1993). The distance from Lemala Gate to the end of the ascent road is 32km and from Seneto Gate to Lemala Gate is 34km.

The rim - plants Along the rim of the Ngorongoro Crater the lush vegetation is very striking. The most common trees are the tall, straight-stemmed Pillarwoods (*Cassipourea malosana*), the majestic Strangler Figs (*Ficus thonningii*), the fluted-stemmed Nuxias (*Nuxia floribunda*), the layered-canopied, compound-leaved Albizia (*Albizia gummifera*) and the grey-stemmed, heart-leaved Croton

(*Croton megalocarpus*). The lichens on the trees belong to the genus *Usnea*. One of the most common shrubs is *Crotalaria agatiflora* with its three leaflets and yellow, pea-like flowers, borne on erect branches towards the top of the plant. Another common shrub is the purple-flowered Vernonia (*Vernonia auriculifera*). This plant has large leaves (up to 70cm long), borne in rosettes at the apex of the branches.

The wild flowering herbs provide a splendour of colour, but yellow seems to be the more dominant. Refer to pg 77 for more details on the vegetation. Some of the most common species are:

*Pillarwood Tree
(Cassipourea malosana)*

*Lichens
(Usnea sp.)*

Strangling Fig
(Ficus thonningii)

Mountain Vernonia
(Vernonia auriculifera)

Nuxia
(Nuxia congesta)

Crotalaria agatiflora

Golden Shower
(Senecio hadiense)

Verbascum
brevipedicellatum

Gynura
(Gynura scandens)

Larkspur
(Delphinium leroy)

Wild Clover
(Trifolia burchellenianum)

Lantana
(Lantana trifolium)

The rim - animals   Buffaloes, especially lone bulls, are commonly seen along the rim. At night one gets the rare opportunity to see bushpigs, as they often visit the camping sites to scavenge. If you look carefully, you might see Tree Hyraxes in the trees. If you don't see them, you may hear them at night - they have a distinctive, screeching call. The Olive Baboon is also commonly seen on the rim and they provide hours of amusement along the roadsides. Do not feed them, no matter how big the temptation. By feeding them, they lose their fear of man and will have to be destroyed if they become a problem.

Olive Baboon   Tree Hyrax

The rim - birds   One of the most common birds of prey is the Augur Buzzard which is either black and white, or (rarely) all black. Look out for the Verreaux's Eagle - a black eagle with a white rump, and which favours mountainous areas. In southern Africa it is known as the Black Eagle. One usually only sees them soaring above but they can be recognised by the fact that they are totally black below, except for the white patches near the wing tips and by the pinched-in wing bases.

Verreaux's Eagle   Augar Buzzard

PLACES TO SEE

PLACES TO SEE

Where to enter the Ngorongoro Crater

There are only two places to enter, at Seneto descent road on the south-western side or at Lemala Gate on the north-eastern side. The road at Seneto is only an entrance but the road at Lemala is both an entrance and an exit. Keep in mind that there is an additional fee of US \$100 per vehicle to be paid when entering the crater. The Ngorongoro Crater is the main tourist attraction in the NCA, so expect many other tourist vehicles. It is advisable to enter as soon as the gates open and to spend the entire day inside the Crater. There are toilet facilities and picnic spots available, so it is ideal to take a packed lunch. The best time to see predator activity is early in the morning.

Animals of the Ngorongoro Crater

The Ngorongoro Crater is often described as a huge zoo because it is so easy to see the animals. The truth is, it is not a zoo, a fact that makes the staggering number and variety of animals even more unique. It is one of only two places where one can see the Black Rhino in its natural habitat in northern Tanzania, the other being at Moru Kopjes in the Serengeti. The Rhinos in these areas are monitored 24h per day to prevent poaching. See the box on pg 35 to read more about the Black Rhino Protection Programme.

The Ngorongoro Crater supports a vast number of animals because of the fresh water that it holds. Most animals that occur in other parts of the NCA also occur in the Ngorongoro Crater. The three ungulates that are conspicuously absent are Impala, Topi and Giraffe. The interesting thing is that the Giraffes are quite capable of walking in and out of the crater but the deterrent seems to be the absence of their favourite food species, *Acacia tortilis* and *A. nilotica* (see pg 108 for more details on the mammals of the Ngorongoro Crater). There is a resident population of animals in the Ngorongoro Crater that varies in number from 20 000 to 25 000. The population seems to remain fairly stable, with seasonal variations. The Wildebeests and

Zebras are the most numerous and their numbers increase during the dry season - the reverse of what happens on the plains. On the other hand, Elephant, Eland and Waterbuck populations tend to increase during the rainy season. Animals move freely in and out of the crater, making use of animal footpaths and cattle tracks, mainly on the western and less steep side. During the rainy season the grazers are spread throughout the crater but during the dry season they concentrate in areas where the grass is green, such as on slope edges and around the Mandusi and Gorigor Swamps.

Coke's Hartebeest in the crater

Descent road

As one comes down the descent road, there are interesting plants to observe, the most imposing being the Candelabra (*Euphorbia candelabrum*) and the Tree Euphorbia (*Euphorbia bussei*). One of the most common shrubs here and along the ascent road is the aromatic Bushman's Tea (*Lippia javanica*), the Poison Apple (*Solanum incanum*) and the Lion's Paw (*Leonotis nepetifolia*). (See pg 83 for details on the vegetation.) On reaching the floor of the crater, one can either turn right to the Lerai Forest or left towards Lake Magadi.

Stay on the roads

Take care not to go off the roads to get closer to the animals. Apart from disturbing the animals, the volcanic soil is very sensitive and a disturbed area will take many seasons to recover. The authorities are trying their best to limit the number of roads. Do adhere to the rules as it is based on a simple fact - the more roads there are, the less grazing there is for the animals and ultimately, the less animals there will be.

The Ngoitokitok picnic site

The picnic site at the base of the ascent road

Which routes to take
The crater is only ±22km in diameter and it is easy to do all the roads in one day. The distance from Lemala Gate to the end of the ascent road is 32km and from Seneto Gate to Lemala Gate is 34km. The wonderful thing about the Ngorongoro Crater is that it offers a different experience every day, no matter how often you go in. Even if you do the same route in one day, it is always different because of animal movements and change of light and cloud formations.

Toilet facilities and picnic sites
There are picnic and toilet facilities near the Lerai Forest and at Ngoitokitok Springs. It is advisable to bring refreshments along as one is allowed to get out of your car at these two places. The Ngoitokitok picnic site it particularly nice as there are hippos in the pool and a great variety of birds, all of which want to share your food. In particular, watch out for the Black Kites that have become very bold, often swooping down to grab a few bites.

Inner circular route
Coming down the descent road, one can turn right to go to the Lerai Forest or left to go on the circular routes. As soon as one turns left, the road forks. If you take the right fork at this point, you will go on the inner circle - the road that skirts the lake. If you go left, you will do the outer circle to Engitati Hill. Early in the morning one often sees Hyenas on the inner circle route and if you are very lucky, you may see Lions doing something else other than sleeping. The rest of the day you will find the Lions in a state of utter relaxation - they will not even move out of the road for vehicles and they will barely spare you a glance. The birdlife is always spectacular around the lake. For photography, a morning and an afternoon drive along the lake shore is advised as the light is favourable at both times.

Lake Makat or Lake Magadi
'Makat' is the Maasai name and 'Magadi' is the Swahili name, both meaning 'soda' or 'salt'. Although it is a salt pan, it is a very important refuge for birds, especially Flamingos. The Flamingos fly in daily, mainly from lake Natron. Flamingos prefer salty waters as they feed on plankton, the latter being the collective name for microscopic plants and animals that occur in saline lakes (see box on pg 57 for more details on Flamingos).

The birdlife on Lake Magadi is fantastic at all times of the year

Goose Ponds The Goose Ponds, west of Lake Magadi, are particularly rewarding in the wet season, allowing close-up photography of the birdlife. However, they are dry for much of the rest of the year.

Engitati Hill One can get an excellent view of the area from Engitati Hill, which looks down on the Mandusi Swamp where Buffalo and Elephant are often seen.

The Mandusi Swamp There are roads crossing the swamp but they are only accessible during the dry season. This is a good place to see Elephant, Buffalo and the rare and shy Bohor Reedbuck. Two of the most common plants growing here are the Giant Sedge (*Cyperus* sp.) and the Swamp-weed (*Aeschynomene schimperi*). This is a pod-plant with pea-like flowers, which grows in marshy areas. It is very high in nutrition, making it a favourite with browsing animals during the dry season.

There are plenty of Hippos to be seen at close range at the Hippo Pool near Mandusi Swamp

Hippo Pool There is always action at the Hippo Pool. Apart from getting the opportunity to watch Hippos at close range, the birdlife is excellent, with Pelicans and Cattle Egrets being some of the more common visitors.

The Munge River Buffalo can often be seen along the Munge River. The river is favoured by wildlife because its water is fresh. When the grass is short, one can see the old German farm ruins just north of the Munge River (see map 7 on pg 26 for location).

Ngoitokitok Springs The Ngoitokitok Springs is a natural spring that starts out as an underground stream on Mount Oldeani and supplies fresh water to the Gorigor Swamp. The water forms a lake or large dam near the spring before disappearing into a swamp. The spring is situated just north-east of the Ngoitokitok picnic site. At the picnic site it forms a dam where Hippos can be seen.

Lerai Forest If you want to see the big tuskers, the Lerai Forest is the place to go. There are no Elephant breeding herds in the crater, only bulls. The breeding herds prefer the forest along the rim. The high nutrient value of the volcanic soils found in the

Giant Sedge (Cyperus sp.)

Swamp-weed (Aeschynomene schimperi)

Cattle Egret   **Great White Pelican**

Ngorongoro Crater and the phosphorous-rich plants it supports, is ideal for the formation of large tusks (see box on right). The Rhinos seem to favour the area between the Lerai Forest and Lake Magadi as well as the area between the Lerai Forest and the Gorigor Swamp. The only one of the big five that is not commonly seen is the Leopard, because of its secretive, nocturnal lifestyle. However, Rhino, Elephant, Buffalo and Lion are almost guaranteed on a day game drive in the Ngorongoro Crater. If you do see Leopard, consider yourself extremely lucky.

The dominant tree in the Lerai Forest is the yellow-barked Fever Tree (*Acacia xanthophloea*). Other trees are the Acacia-like Ana Tree (*Faedherbia albida*, previously *Acacia albida*). The Ana Tree bears its leaves and pods in winter, making it an important species for browsing animals in the dry season. As one crosses the streams in the Lerai Forest, there are beautiful specimens of the Quinine Tree (*Rauvolfia caffra*). It is an attractive evergreen tree with yellowish-brown, corky bark and whorls of three to five shiny, leathery leaves. All parts of the tree exude a toxic, milky latex but a bark infusion is nevertheless used as a powerful medicine to disinfect external wounds and to treat coughs. Because of its potency, it is very effective in killing maggots in external wounds.

HOW IVORY IS FORMED

Ivory is a non-cellular substance secreted by cells on the outer surface of a highly vascular pulp cavity which is the 'living core' of the Elephant tusk. The substance is transported via microscopic tubes (tubules) that reach into the existing tooth material. The tubules are responsible for the laying down of dentine as well as for the characteristic cross-grained matrix of Elephant tusks.

The dentine laid down by the tubules consists of 20% organic material and 80% inorganic material. The organic material consists of fibrous protein, mostly collagen. The inorganic material consists of oxygen, hydrogen, calcium and phosphorous. The high mineral and phosphorous quality of volcanic soils, and the mineral-rich plants they support, account for the large tuskers that one can still see in the Ngorongoro Crater. In contrast, Elephants in Botswana have exceptionally small tusks as a direct result of the low phosphorous quality of the soils and the plants.

The pulp cavity is supplied with numerous blood vessels and fine nerves, explaining why a badly fractured or broken tusk can cause severe pain to the Elephant and cause it to be extremely aggressive. Tusks grow at a rate of ±11cm per year for males and 8,5cm per year for females (Laws, 1970).

Lerai Forest

The Elephant bulls in the Ngorongoro Crater have exceptionally large tusks

PLACES TO SEE

33

Gorigor Swamp One cannot approach too closely to this swamp but there is a pool where one can view Hippos and Pelicans and many other water birds. Rhinos can also often be seen here as well as the Defassa Waterbuck.

Defassa Waterbuck

Wild flowers and grasses When visiting during the rains, the crater floor is dramatically streaked with yellow and purple. The dominant yellow flowers are mostly *Bidens taitensis, Bidens schimperi* and *Aspilia mossambicensis*, while the purple ones are mainly *Gutenbergia cordifolia*. Although very striking in their colourful splendour, the abundance of flowers is not a good reflection on the state of the grass cover - the more flowers there are, the less grass there is. Flowers tend to take over after severe droughts or over-grazing.

The main grass species that occurs in the open areas in the crater is Oats Grass (*Themeda triandra*). In the swampy areas it is mainly the rusty-coloured Rhodes Grass (*Chloris gayana*) and Thatching Grass (*Hyparrhenia rufa*). Around the pans, the most saline resistant of all is *Odyssea* sp., which grows closest to the pans, followed by Spike Grass (*Sporobolus spicatus*) and then by Couch Grass (*Cynodon dactylon*).

Ascent road The ascent road is an experience in itself. It gives you a healthy adrenaline rush because of the height and the sheer cliffs - more so when the road is wet! Allow enough time to take it slowly, enjoying the scenery and the plants along the road. It is always fun to look at beautiful wild flowers but it becomes a whole new experience when you try to identify them as you travel along. You will soon find that the same plants recur at regular intervals and it is easy to learn the most common species (see pg 77 for more details of the plants and their uses).

Aspilia mossambicencis   *Gutenbergia cordifolia*

The yellow flowers on the crater floor belong mainly to the genera Bidens and Aspilia

THE BLACK RHINO PROTECTION PROGRAM

There are five species of Rhino in the world, of which two species are found in Africa - the White Rhino and the Black Rhino. Tanzania has two of the last remaining free-ranging Black Rhino populations in east Africa - one in the Ngorongoro Crater and the other in the Moru Kopjes in the Serengeti National Park.

In 1966 there were 108 Rhinos in the Ngorongoro Crater - about one Rhino per 3,1km². In the Olduvai Gorge 69 Rhinos were counted at this time.

Between 1974 and 1978 an estimated 700 Black Rhinos occurred in the SNP. Around the Seronera River there was a rich density of one Rhino per 10km².

After 1975 Rhino poaching became a serious problem in northern Tanzania. Demand for Rhino horn on the world market increased, not only for medicine and its use as an aphrodisiac, but also in North Yemen, where horns are carved into dagger handles. With the increase in demand, prices increased and so did the ruthlessness of poachers.

In 1980 there were an estimated 50 to 100 Rhinos left in the Serengeti National Park, of which the only viable population was at Moru Kopjes - a mere 20 animals. During this time the Ngorongoro Rhinos have declined from 108 in 1966 to about 30 animals in 1980. Not a single Rhino survived in the Olduvai Gorge area. A huge effort was made to reduce poaching, but it was not stopped.

In 1993 there was a further decline and only 14 to 18 Rhinos were counted in the Ngorongoro Crater. Isolated individuals survived in the Serengeti (only an estimated five animals). The once common Black Rhino was now almost extinct in northern Tanzania. It was time for drastic steps.

In November 1993 the Ngorongoro Conservation Area Authority (NCAA) and the Frankfurt Zoological Society (FZS) jointly devised a project for the conservation of Rhinos in the Ngorongoro Crater - The Black Rhino Protection Programme. Some 13 Rhinos were counted - two adult males, six adult females and five immature animals. In 1994 a sub-adult male, Rajabu, emigrated to the Moru Kopjes and met up with two adult females. In 1995 a similar joint project was initiated between Tanzania National Parks (TANAPA) and the FZS.

In May 2000 the Rhino population of the Ngorongoro Crater had increased to 17 animals even though three were lost to natural causes and one female to poaching. Currently there are about 20 Rhinos in the crater. The Moru Kopjes population had increased to seven animals in 2000. Although there is still a long way to go, these joint projects have certainly proved very successful thanks to the commitment of the NCAA, TANAPA, the FZS and the dedication of the rangers and researchers involved in the project.

Today each Rhino is equipped with a tracking device which is implanted in its horn. They are guarded 24 hours a day.

Tracking devices are implanted in the horns

Today, Black Rhino sightings are almost 100% guaranteed in the Ngorongoro Crater

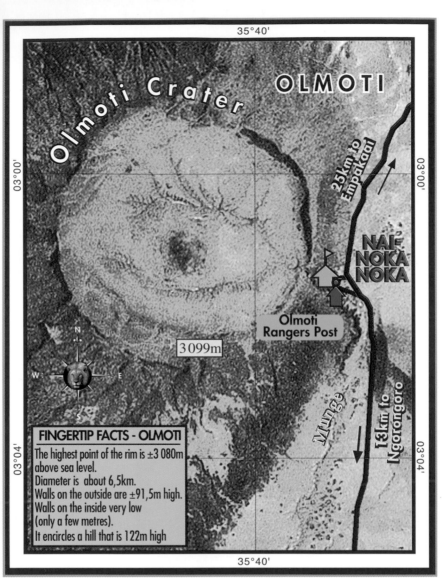

35°40'

O l m o t i   C r a t e r   OLMOTI

03°00'

25km to Empakaai

NAI NOKA NOKA

Olmoti Rangers Post

3 099m

03°00'

N
W — E
S

13km to Ngorongoro

Munge

03°04'

FINGERTIP FACTS - OLMOTI

The highest point of the rim is ±3 080m above sea level.
Diameter is about 6,5km.
Walls on the outside are ±91,5m high.
Walls on the inside very low (only a few metres).
It encircles a hill that is 122m high

03°04'

35°40'

Satellite image of Olmoti Crater

MAP 9

A typical scence in the Olmoti area

Nainokanoka Village at the foot of Olmoti Crater

Take note: To visit Olmoti Crater one can drive to Nainokanoka Village at the foot of Olmoti Crater, where you can meet up with a guide at the Rangers Post who will take you to the rim.

Olmoti is situated on the northern side of the Ngorongoro Crater. One can get there by driving along the rim or through the Ngorongoro Crater to Lemala Gate. Almost directly after the gate, one turns right onto the road to Empakaai. From the Lemala Gate, travel for 13km to Nainokanoka Village. The last track going left will take you to the Rangers Post where you can leave your car while a guide walks you to the summit.

The Olmoti Crater is one of the major water catchment areas in the Ngorongoro Highlands. The vegetation and the soils act as a sponge, absorbing and filtering the water, thus rendering it fresh. The filtered water plunges over a weakness in the crater wall, forming a beautiful waterfall of about 100m high. The fresh water is transported via the Munge River into the Mandusi Swamp and eventually into Lake Magadi inside the Ngorongoro Crater. Lake Magadi, however, is a salt lake. Olmoti is also an important water source for the residents and livestock of Nainokanoka Village at the foot of this crater.

It is not a long climb to the rim, only between 30 and 45 minutes, but keep in mind that one is almost at 3 000m, so take the climb slowly. The view is not as beautiful as at Empakaai, as the caldera is shallow in comparison and it does not form a lake at the bottom. It is well worth the walk to Munge Gorge where the waterfall is. This is the actual source of the Munge Stream in the Ngorongoro Crater. From here one has a beautiful view of the Embulbul Depression when looking in the direction of Empakaai. The Embulbul Depression is the low-lying area surrounded by the slopes of Olmoti, Empakaai, Losirua and Lolmalasin. The highest point at Olmoti is 3 080m and the crater is about 6,5km in diameter. The prominent hill on the eastern side of Olmoti Crater is called Endoinyo Wuass.

PLACES TO SEE

LOSIRUA AND LOLMALASIN CRATERS

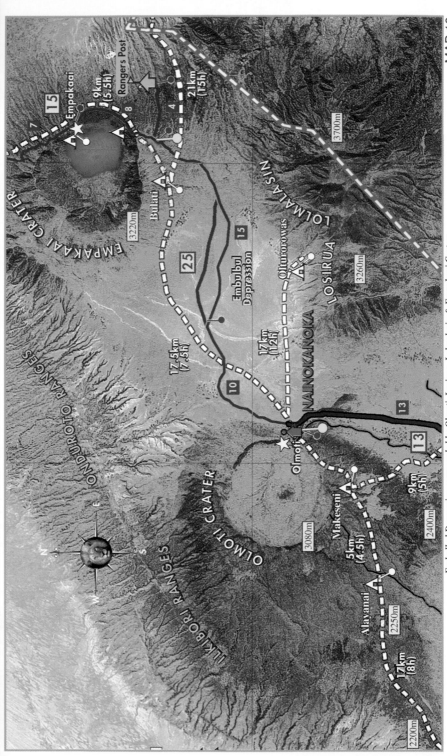

Embulbul Depression surrounded by Olmoti, Losirua, Lolmalasin & Empakaai Craters

MAP 10

EMPAKAAI CRATER

Empakaai

9km
(5.5h)

Rangers Post

21km
(15h)

Bulati

3220m

3700m

LOLMALASIN

Embulbul
Depression

Olkuruwas

3260m

LOSIRUA

NAINOKANOKA

ONDUROTO RANGES

17.5km
(7.5h)

17km
(12h)

Olmoti

OLMOTI CRATER

3080m

Makeseni

9km
(5h)

2400m

ILKIBORI RANGES

5km
(4.5h)

Alayanai

2250m

17km
(8h)

2200m

*The Embulbul Depression with the merged Losirua and Lolmalasin Craters in the background
- the highest point in the NCA at 3700m -*

When travelling to Empakaai one passes through the Embulbul Depression - a rather long and monotonous stretch of road (25km from Olmoti to Empakaai). Take note that this road becomes very muddy in the rainy season. To the south (your right) you will see what looks like a very large mountain. It is, in fact, two merged craters, Losirua and Lolmalasin, the two highest craters in the Ngorongoro Highlands. The lower summit is Losirua and and the higher is Lolmalasin. Losirua reaches 3 260m, while Lolmalasin forms the highest point in the Ngorongoro Highlands at 3 700m above sea level. The floor of the Embulbul Depression is at 2 320m, which is relatively high, considering that the highest point of the Ngorongoro rim is 2 359m. There are many Maasai villages in the Embulbul Depression and one can see cattle, goats and wildlife roaming side by side in absolute harmony.

As soon as one starts to ascend, the vegetation becomes more interesting. About 25km after Nainokanoka Village, you will reach a T-junction which is only ±3km from the rim of the crater. If you want to go to Empakaai, turn left here. The road to the right leads to the Empakaai Rangers Post.

Masaai at Embulbul Depression

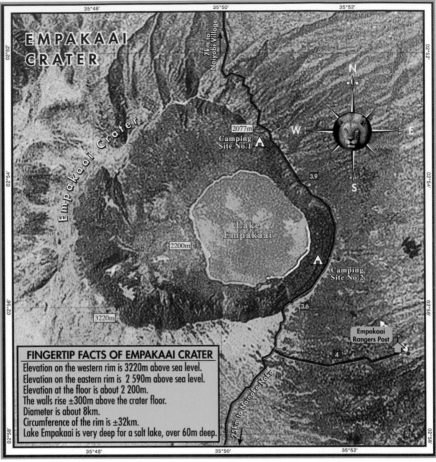

EMPAKAAI CRATER

FINGERTIP FACTS OF EMPAKAAI CRATER
Elevation on the western rim is 3220m above sea level.
Elevation on the eastern rim is 2 590m above sea level.
Elevation at the floor is about 2 200m.
The walls rise ±300m above the crater floor.
Diameter is about 8km.
Circumference of the rim is ±32km.
Lake Empakaai is very deep for a salt lake, over 60m deep.

Satellite image of Empakaai Crater

MAP 11

Take note: *If you wish to visit Empakaai, it is necessary to get a guide at the tourist office at Ngorongoro.*

The Empakaai Rangers Post If you turn right at the T-junction mentioned on the previous page, you will descend to the Rangers Post on a road that tunnels its way through lush, evergreen mountain forest. The Rangers Post is in a beautiful setting almost at the edge of the escarpment. There is a school at the site and the children are delightful. You can leave your car here and walk a few hundred metres to the east to enjoy a spectacular view of the Gregory Rift Valley and Kerimasi Crater.

The road that tunnels its way to the Empakaai Rangers Post

The Empakaai Crater

The view of the Gregory Rift Valley from just beyond the Empakaai Rangers Post.
Notice the Keramasi Crater on the left of the photograph

If one turns left at the T-junction mentioned previously, the road will lead you to the Empakaai Crater. One of the most prominent trees one notices on this road is *Hygenia abyssinica* which occurs almost exclusively above 2 800m and is therefore not seen along the Ngorongoro Crater rim. It has drooping, feathery leaves and the flowers form masses of bright pink to red drooping clusters at the top of the tree, the female flowers being brighter in colour than the male flowers. The other common trees in the area are *Nuxia floribunda* which is easily recognisable by its fluted tree-trunks, *Ficus natalensis* with its entangled aerial roots and *Croton macrostachyus* with its heart-shaped leaves and light-grey bark. There is also a stretch of the red-flowered herb, *Leonotis nepetifolia,* with its globular, red-flowered flowerheads. Sunbirds love this plant, the most common in the area being the spectacular, metallic green, Scarlet-tufted Malachite Sunbird with its curved bill and long tail.

Empakaai Crater Empakaai is arguably the most beautiful place in the entire NCA, so brace yourself for unimaginable scenery. The elevation on the western rim is 3 200m above sea level and on the eastern rim (where the road is) it is 2 590m above sea level. The elevation at the floor is about 2 200m. The wall rises ±300m above the crater floor and the crater is about 8km in diameter. The circumference of the rim is ±32km but currently, the road follows only the eastern side of the rim. Because of the high altitude, the area is often shrouded in mist and combined with the emerald colour of the lake, it creates an atmosphere straight out of a fairy tale!

There are camps on the eastern rim where one can spend the night or leave your car and get a guide to take you down the wall to the lake. It is only a 30 to 50 minute walk down and slightly longer to climb back up. One may see game - even Buffalo. You should carry some water down as the lake is saline. Remember to climb slowly as the elevation is very high, up to 3 200m on the opposite side. The nights are very cold in winter and when it rains in summer, the wind becomes freezing cold.

If you are a plant lover, you are literally in paradise - at least that is how I experienced it when I first saw Empakaai. The plants of this region are discussed on pg 95 under 'Vegetation' but the following are some of the most commonly seen species:

The Scarlet-tufted Malachite Sunbird sucking nectar from Leonotis nepetifolia

Gladiolus natalensis

Kniphofia thomsonii

Pavonia urens

Leonotis mollisama

Hygenia abyssinica is one of the most common trees seen as one approaches Empakaai Crater

Lake Empakaai Lake Empakaai is situated in the Empakaai Crater. Like the Ngorongoro and Olmoti Craters, Empakaai is also a caldera, with the difference being that a large portion of its floor is covered in water. The water takes on an emerald to turquoise to deep-blue colour, depending on the thickness of the clouds and the angle of the light - hence the alternative name of 'Emerald Crater'. The water is often lined with pale pink - the result of thousands of Flamingoes that congregate there to feed during the day, returning to their nesting sites at night, mainly at Lake Natron. Although Lake Empakaai is a salt lake, it is said to be over 61m deep in places - extremely deep for a salt lake. Its depth accounts partly for its iridescent colour.

PLACES TO SEE

Empakaai Crater with Oldoinyo Lengai in the backround

The western shore of Lake Empakaai

The camping site at Empakaai Crater

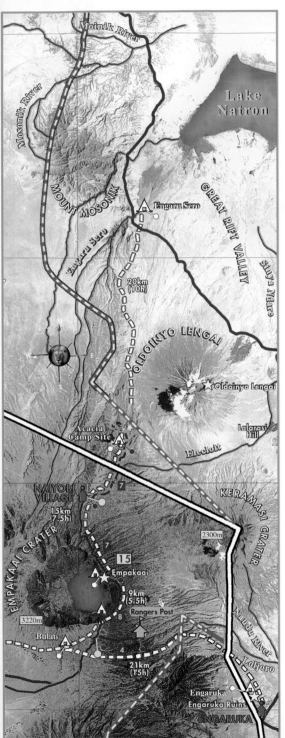

Empakaai, Kerimasi, Oldoinyo Lengai, Mosonik & Lake Natron MAP 12

On the northern side of Empakaai Crater, one can continue to Naiyobi Village where the road ends. Even from the rim of Empakaai one can see Oldoinyo Lengai looming in the distance, but if you follow the cattle tracks beyond Naiyobi for a stretch to the north, the top part of Oldoinyo Lengai will suddenly appear infront of you - larger than life. There are thousands of Cattle, Goats and Donkeys, all of which have created a maze of highways and byways that criss-cross the area. This is not a very favourable situation for erosion control, but to see the red-clad Maasai herdsmen returning their livestock at dusk, stirring up dust against the red sunset, is a sight not easily forgotten!

Oldoinyo Lengai was formed during the formation of the Gregory Rift and became active when Kerimasi ceased to do so (600 000 - 370 000 million years ago). It is situated just north of the NCA on the valley floor. The elevation at the summit is 2878m above sea level and the elevation of the valley floor is ±1000m, making it about 1880m high.

'Oldoinyo Lengai' means 'Mountain of God' - so named because of its religious significance to the Maasai. Even today the Maasai still climb up the crater to pray. Oldoinyo Lengai is still active with a long history of recorded eruptions. The first scientific description of the mountain was made in 1883 by G.A. Fischer.

Oldoinyo Lengai as seen from Acacia camp site beyond Naiyobi Village

He reported 'smoke' rising from the summit and rumbling noises heard by local inhabitants. The first major eruption that was officially documented took place in 1917 and lasted from January to June of that year. Ash was deposited up to 55km away. It was this eruption that destroyed the formerly luxuriant vegetation on the lower slopes. Subsequent eruptions took place in 1926 and 1940. During the latter eruption the ash was so heavy that it rendered the grazing on the Salei Plains and the Gol Mountain area inedible to wildlife and cattle, causing the Maasai to migrate to other areas. The westward winds carried the ash as far west as Banagi. In 1966 another major eruption was reported and in 1983 rumblings were observed. The most recent eruption was recorded on the night of 24th March 2006 and it continued rumbling and spitting lava for more than a week. The dried up magma was observed through a radius of 3km afterwards. No human lives were claimed but it caused about 3000 local inhabitants to flee. Interestingly, Oldoinyo Lengai is the only volcano in the world that emits natrocarbonatite lava which is highly fluid and contains almost no silicon. It is almost black in colour or looks like brown foam, depending how much gas is present. This kind of lava is much cooler than basaltic lavas, measuring about 510°C (950°F), compared to over 1100°C (2000°F) for basaltic lavas.

It is possible to climb up the active volcano to have a closer look, but this needs to be organised and booked ahead of time (see pg 22 for details on walking trails).

When facing Oldoinyo Lengai you will see Lake Natron beyond, which is situated at 610m above sea level. More to the left (west), you will get a bird's-eye view of the the extinct volcano, Mosonik, which protrudes from the surrounding plains and is clearly recognisable by its saw-toothed profile.

A view of the extinct crater - Mosonik - with its saw-toothed profile

GOL MOUNTAINS

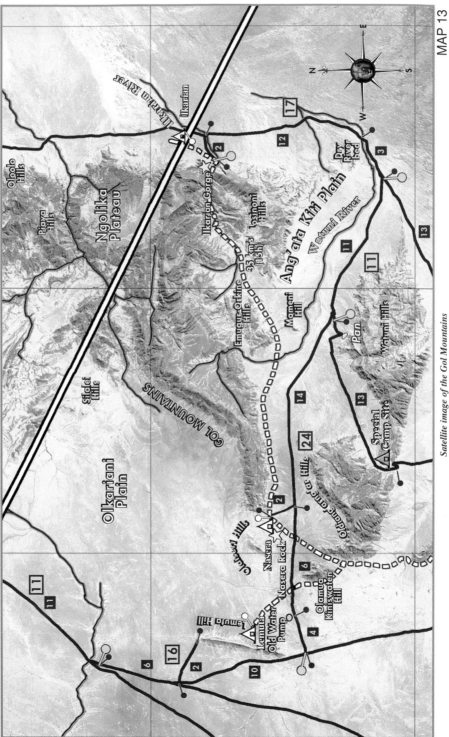

Satellite image of the Gol Mountains

MAP 13

The Gol Mountains as seen from the eastern side

As one drives north along the Malambo road, there are many beautiful views of the Gol Mountains. One can almost imagine the events that caused the formation of the Great Rift Valley (see pg 69 for details). The Malambo road follows the general area where a huge fracture developed in the earth's crust about 20 million years ago. This caused the area east of the Gol Mountains as well as the eastern part of the mountains to sag between 900m and 1800m. Subsequently, fluid lava and layers of volcanic ash filled up the area to form the Sale Plain. The Gol Mountains were much higher originally, but its base is buried under layers of volcanic ash. Erosion over thousands of years caused the edges of the mountain to soften and valleys were formed, resulting in the beautiful scenery that we see today.

PLACES TO SEE

Ilkarian Gorge

Take note: *The Gol Mountain area can only be visited when accompanied by a guide, which must be organised at the tourist office at Ngorongoro. There is a spectacular walking trail that passes all along the Ilkarian Gorge, which is highly recommended (see pg 22 for details on walking trails.)*

Ilkarian Gorge is ecologically important because it is a vital nesting site of the Rueppell's Griffon Vulture. To get there one turns north (right when coming from Ngorongoro Crater) onto the Malambo road. This turn-off is 24km from the Ngorongoro Crater Entrance Gate and 7km before you reach the Olduvai Gorge turn-off. This road passes just west of the Olbalbal Swamp. One crosses the Olduvai Gorge after 10km and another small gorge after a further 17km. The road then bends north-east until it nears the Gol Mountain range. At 39km from the main road one reaches the Nasera Rock turn-off to the west (left). This road is not easy to see but it basically follows the foot of the mountain range along the Ang'ata Kiti Plain. Ignore this road and carry on straight (north). As one approaches Ilkarian, Mosonik, the extinct volcano with its saw-toothed profile, becomes visible to your right. On a clear day you can see Oldoinyo Lengai further to the right.

The Ilkarian Gorge is very narrow in places

Just 15km beyond the turn-off to Nasera Rock you cross the Ilkarian River, directly after which you turn left and continue for 2km until you reach Ilkarian Gorge. Park your car a distance from the gorge in the allocated parking area so as not to disturb the Vultures. Be sure to take your camera as the view at the mouth of the gorge is spectacular, the walls barely two metres apart in places. If you want to photograph the vultures, you will need a large lens.

To see the vultures soaring above going about their everyday activities, to me, was an almost spiritual experience. It makes one feel rather insignificant as you witness a natural phenomenon that has remained unchanged by human influence for centuries.

The best time to visit Ilkarian is from March to April when the vultures are breeding. This coincides with the migration when there is plenty of food available. Vultures have the tendency to gorge themselves during times like this, often to the point where they are unable to fly. During the research for this travel guide, I had the opportunity to witness this first-hand. A magnificent specimen of a Rueppell's Griffon failed to fly away as my vehicle approached. It made a few failed attempts but then I sensed its obvious discomfort. Without any warning it heaved once or twice and regurgitated a huge amount of chunky, slimy meat matter. I have never before or since encountered a smell so vile! After this it immediately took off without any effort - and so did I! As I drove away I reflected on how important vultures are to the

Rueppell's Griffon Vulture seconds after it lightened its load by regurgitating its food

ecosystem. Without their ability to clean up after predators, harmful bacteria, viruses and parasites would multiply and proliferate, ultimately causing disease that could wipe out entire species. Read more about vultures in the box below.

INTERESTING FACTS ABOUT VULTURES

There are eight species of vulture in Tanzania. They are:

Rueppell's Griffon	White-backed Vulture
Hooded Vulture	Lappet-faced Vulture
White-headed Vulture	Egyptian Vulture
Bearded Vulture	Palmnut Vulture

Of these, the Rueppell's, White-backed, Hooded, Lappet-faced and White-headed Vultures are regularly seen in the NCA and all five of them breed in the area.

ANATOMY OF VULTURES

Feet A vulture's feet are flat compared to that of an eagle because they spend so much time on the ground. Their talons (claws) are thick and sharp, with the exception of the Rueppell's Griffon, which spends much of its time on cliffs, causing the talons to be blunt.

Bill The bill consists of keratin and is produced by the epidermis of the skin, growing throughout life. Feeding keeps the bill tip worn down.

Tongue In the Rueppell's Griffon the tongue is strongly grooved, each groove being sharply serrated with 'teeth-like' protrusions pointing backward. The bone in the tongue of the Griffon is also larger than in other vultures. It uses the tongue to facilitate fast swallowing by pushing the food down its throat. The Bearded Vulture feeds mainly on bones and bone marrow. Its tongue is also grooved but not serrated, ideal for extracting bone marrow. The Bearded Vulture has a very wide gape, enabling it to swallow bones.

Starvation Vultures have to go without food for long periods of time. Experiments have shown that White-backed Vultures can last without food for 14 days, while experts say that they could probably last up to 20 days.

Vision During certain seasons, vultures rely almost entirely on their vision to locate food. Experiments have shown that they can see an object as small as 6,4cm in diameter from about 1km up in the air.

They soar at different levels, forming foraging 'nets'. The birds lower down usually spot the food first and then the birds higher up simply follow them down. The White-headed Vulture is often first at a carcass. It has not been established if their eye-sight is superior to that of other vultures, but they do have the largest external eye size of the group.

Smell Most African vultures do not rely on their sense of smell to locate food but it has been proven that the Turkey Vulture (which occurs in the Americas) uses its excellent sense of smell to locate carcasses in the dense, forest habitat that it favours.

Salt excretion Unlike mammals, bird kidneys are not well developed and are not efficient in excreting salt. The nostrils take over this function. Because of the high salt content of the meat they feed on, vultures secrete copious amounts of saline nasal fluid whilst feeding. This can be seen if you watch carefully.

Necks Vultures have long necks to enable them to feed inside a carcass. The species with the longest necks also have the barest necks, to prevent the feathers from becoming soiled. All vultures have between 15 and 17 neck vertebrae. The Griffon, which has 17, can thrust its neck ±50cm into a carcass. Accounts from vulture handlers confirm that the neck of a Griffon is by far the most powerful.

Crop The crop of a vulture is really just a temporary storage organ. It is a distensible sack on the front of the oesophagus. Polite feeding manners are not in a vulture's nature, and the aim of all vultures is to fill the crop as quickly as possible. No digestion takes place in the crop, but the food can be easily regurgitated to a nestling, or if a vulture finds that it cannot fly because of the heavy load. A Griffon's crop can take ±1,5kg - that is about 16% to 20% of the bird's body weight. This is the equivalent of a 70kg man eating 14kg of meat in one meal! To give the reader a better idea, the average Thomson's Gazelle weighs between 19 and 25kg and the Kirk's Dik-dik weighs only 5kg.

Digestion Digestion takes place in the stomach. A full crop of food takes a long time to digest, about 30 to 42 hours, mainly because of the small size of the stomach in comparison with the crop. Vultures swallow hair whilst feeding but get rid of it by regurgitating pellets. In the case of a Griffon, the pellets can be almost the size of a tennis ball.

RUEPPELL'S GRIFFON

The Ilkarian Gorge breeding colony The Rueppell's Griffon weighs about 7,5kg with a wingspan of ±2,4m. The breeding colony at Ilkarian in the Gol Mountains, is estimated to be about 2 000 pairs, along 25km of escarpment. Together with the young, this may amount to more than 5 000 birds. Since the Rueppell's Griffon prefers to spend the night on cliffs, they sometimes have to travel far to get to their food source. In the Ngorongoro Conservation Area and the Serengeti, they usually frequent the area where the bulk of the migration is. Colin Pennycuick, who did a study of the colony at Ilkarian, noted that the Griffons can travel up to 140km to get to the migration if necessary. This journey takes up to three hours at an average speed of 47kph. To make travelling easier, the birds make use of so-called 'thermal streets'.

Thermals and thermal streets The most common method employed by vultures to rise in flat savanna country is by means of thermals. Thermal air currents are formed when the sun heats the ground which in turn heats the air above it. This causes the air to rise and create a kind of 'air bubble', almost in the shape of a mushroom. When the 'bubbles' merge, they form upward spirals which we sometimes observe as whirlwinds or 'dust devils'. Thermal streets are formed where hot air currents are produced in one area, move upward and then drift downwind to form an air 'tunnel' or 'thermal street'.

PLACES TO SEE

Pennycuick reports that he followed such a line of thermals in his glider for 47km and even experienced a rise in altitude of ±100m. He found that the Griffons reach speeds of up to 75kph in a straight downward glide.

When wind blows against a mountain or cliff, it creates an air wave on the leeward side of the hill that goes straight up, sometimes to very high altitudes. Vultures often use these waves to gain height.

Air temperatures in rising air decline faster than in still air - about 10°C per kilometre. At about 4km above ground level, temperatures are freezing (0°C). There is a recorded incident where a pilot collided with a Rueppell's Griffon at 11 280m over the Ivory Coast. Temperatures at these altitudes are about -50°C and there is virtually no oxygen. Above 9 150m there are jet streams present - very strong winds. It was surmised that the Griffon was probably sailing along a jet stream when it collided with the aircraft.

It was found that Griffons (probably other high-flying birds too), have specialised haemoglobins to carry more oxygen and together with the anatomy of their lungs and certain cardiovascular adaptations, they are able to survive in such hypoxic (low oxygen) situations.

Breeding Griffons mate for life. They lay only one egg and the incubation period is about 55 days. Both sexes incubate the egg, exchanging places about twice per day. Research at Ilkarian has shown that there may be a shift in breeding times. One study in 1969 reported peak breeding during December and January, while a 1985 study noted peak breeding for August. It is even possible that they have two peaks, but much research is still needed in this regard. The rearing period of the young is about five months and the parents do not remain with their young after they have left the nest. Young birds tend to form groups of their own.

| Rueppell's Griffon | White-backed Vulture | Hooded Vulture |

| White-headed Vulture | Lappet-faced Vulture | Bearded Vulture (Lammergeier) |

SAN PARKS

The Wildebeest and the trees at the base give a good indication of the size of Nasera Rock

Nasera Rock   Nasera Rock is a huge monolith of about 100m high, situated on the western side of the Gol Mountains. To get there, one can approach from Olduvai Gorge by taking the main road north-west, past the Shifting Sand Dunes, that leads to Loliondo. Look for the turn-off to your right (which leads to Nasera Rock) about 26km from Olduvai. The turn-off is just before you reach Lemala Hills. Alternatively, one can take the Malambo road to Ilkarian Gorge and turn west onto the Ang'ata Kiti Plain. Drive along this road for 25km and long before you get there, you will see Nasera Rock in the distance on your right. The third route is straight north from Olduvai Gorge where one actually drives through a dry river bed and a gap in the Gol Mountains to get to the Ang'ata Kiti Plain.   Be careful not to try and cross the riverbed where it is too deep, rather go further downhill to the south where it becomes shallower. This is the most interesting route to take to Nasera. The distance from Olduvai to Nasera Rock via this route is 53km.

Nasera Rock was used during the Stone Age as a shelter. An abundance of bone material and artifacts have been recovered, some of which date back to 30 000 BC. Do take note that this is an archaeological site, and objects may not be removed.

Scenically, Nasera Rock is one of the highlights of the NCA. Imagine a giant rock jutting out from the plains below, like an enormous statue.   Its rock faces are shear, but it is possible to climb to the top from the eastern side, which has a gentler slope. At the base are huge Acacia Trees, dwarfed by the size of the rock.   The name 'Nasera' is a Maasai word referring to the light streaks in the rock.

The Maasai herders often take their goats there to browse and it never ceases to amaze one how the goats do not loose their balance whilst nimbly executing their death-defying antics on the rock. It is also interesting to watch their interaction with the Baboons that have made this rock their home. The Baboons try to show their superiority, but Goats are not easily bossed around. Having Baboons there as sentinels is quite reassuring as they 'bark' at any sign of danger, such as predators or even humans. If you look carefully, you may also see the shy, rock-dwelling antelope - the Klipspringer - on the rocks (see box below). If you visit Nasera during the rainy season, January to February, you may also find yourself surrounded by millions of Wildebeest and Zebra - a truly amazing experience!

THE KLISPRINGER ANTELOPE

The Klipspringer's hooves are tiny and stiletto-like - literally the size of your two little fingers held together. They are rubbery below to ensure that it does not slip whilst jumping from rock to rock. Unlike other antelope, the Klipspringer's eyes are situated more to the front of its head than on the side. This gives it binocular vision much like humans and other primates, enabling it to judge distance.

A male Klipspringer

A storm building up at Nasera Rock

PLACES TO SEE

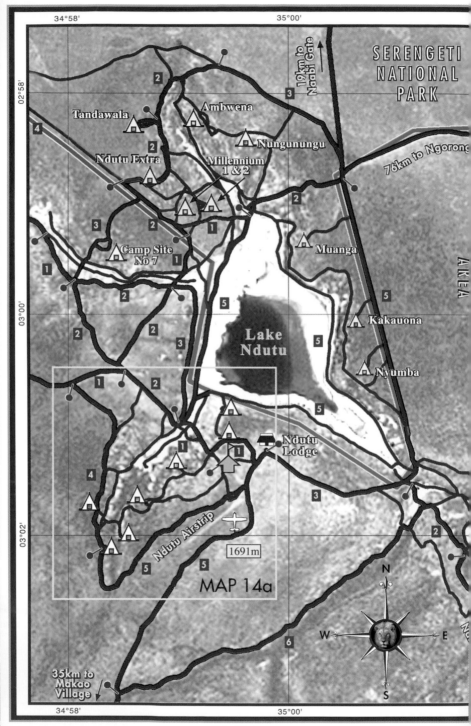

Lake Ndutu

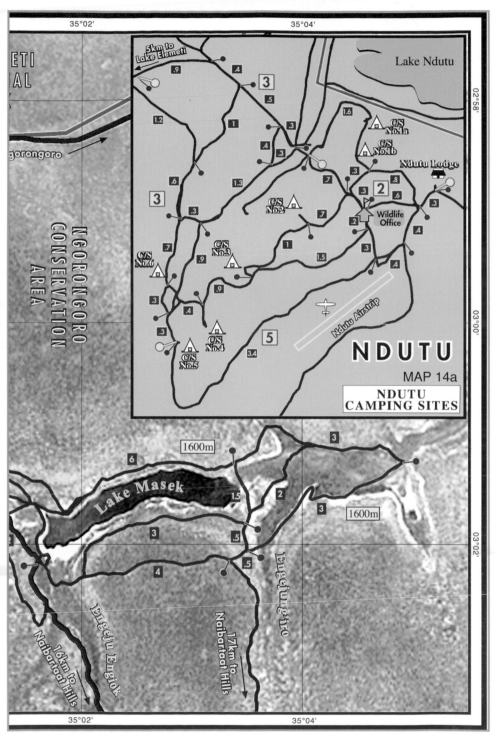

5km to
Lake Elemeti

Lake Ndutu

SERENGETI
NATIONAL
PARK

Ngorongoro

NGORONGORO
CONSERVATION
AREA

.9

3

.4

.5

1.2

1

.3

1.6

C/S
No.1a

.4

C/S
No.1b

.3

Ndutu Lodge

.3

3

.6

1.3

.3

.7

.8

2

.6

3

.3

3

.3

C/S
No.2

7

.7

Wildlife
Office

.2

.4

7

C/S
No.3

.9

1

.3

C/S
No.6

.9

1.5

.4

.3

.4

Ndutu Airstrip

NDUTU

MAP 14a

**NDUTU
CAMPING SITES**

3

C/S
No.4

3.4

5

C/S
No.5

1600m

3

6

Lake Masek

1.5

2

3

1600m

3

.5

4

.5

Engelungiro

16km to
Naibartaat Hills

Engelu Engiok

17km to
Naibartaat Hills

02°58'

03°00'

03°02'

Lake Masek   **MAP 14**

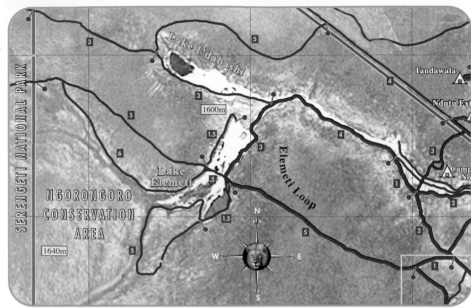

Lake Ndutu - western side

MAP 14b

Lake Ndutu

Wildebeests stampeding across the Lake

Lake Ndutu

Lake Ndutu (also called Lagarja) and Lake Masek form shallow basins where water accumulates from the nearby areas of slightly higher altitude. The water in both lakes is extremely saline, too saline for human consumption, but the animals do sometimes drink there. Most of the water evaporates during the dry season. These two lakes are part of the drainage system to the east, where they drain into the Olbalbal Depression via the Olduvai Gorge. Lake Ndutu becomes alive with animals during the migration because it is surrounded by the Ndutu Woodlands and the Short Grass Plains, which provide ample cover and food.

Wildebeest stampede One of the most exhilarating and heart-rending experiences, is to watch the Wildebeest stampede - a phenomenon that can be triggered by anything, usually predators.

The Wildebeests invariably take the shortest route across the shallow lake to get to the opposite side. In the madness of the moment, calves get separated from their mothers and as soon as the mothers realise, they turn back, creating a two-way chaos within a cacophony of calls.

Without exception, a few calves lose their mothers forever. Lost calves will follow any moving object, especially moving vehicles, and will even walk up to predators. To witness their aggressive rejection by other females and to listen to their forlorn cries, is very touching. The calves often lose all hope and wait motionless in the water until they fall over and die. This is nature's way of eliminating the weakest and preparing the survivors for the even harsher realities of their journey up north.

FLAMINGOS

What attracts Flamingos to salty lakes? Flamingos are very common at the lakes in the NCA, all of which are saline. Flamingos are filter feeders and feed on plankton. Plankton is a collective name for microscopic plants and animals that occur in the mud and on the surface of shallow, saline lakes.

How are they adapted to feed?
The Flamingo's bill is heavy, sharply curved with a deep, trough-like upper mandible and a small, lid-like lower mandible. Whilst feeding, they immerse and invert the bill so that the trough is at the bottom and the lid on top. The thick tongue moves at a fast rate of three to four times per second in the lower mandible to create a pumping action. This action sucks water into the bill. The bill is equipped with very fine, specialised filtering lamellae which allow only the microscopic plankton through. At the same time the Flamingo employs a shuffling foot movement to stir up the plankton in the mud and water (Newman,1979).

Food preferences of Greater and Lesser Flamingoes
It is of interest to note that there is a difference in the food taken in by Greater and Lesser Flamingoes. The Lesser Flamingo is essentially a surface feeder, preferring blue-green algae and diatoms, whilst the Greater Flamingo selects slightly larger organisms such as small mollusks and crustacea. In Lake Magadi, *Saliginella*, a blue-green algae is so common that it constitutes almost the entire diet of the Lesser Flamingo.

Greater Flamingos

Lesser Flamingo

PLACES TO SEE

57

Cultural bomas

NCAA

One can visit the Maasai Cultural Bomas in the NCA to learn more about their unique culture, to take photographs and to buy mementos. There is an entrance fee to be paid but it is well worth it.

Please be sensitive to the fact that it is considered very bad manners to take photographs of people along the roadside without consent. A visit to one of the following bomas is highly recommended:

Kiloki Senyati Cultural Boma is situated on the main road to Serengeti, 7km south-west of the Olduvai Gorge Information Centre.

Loongoku Cultural Boma is situated on the main road to Serengeti, 10km before the turn-off to Olduvai Gorge.

Irkeepus Cultural Boma is situated 2km north-east of Lemala Gate, on the main road to Empakaai.

Seneto Cultural Boma is situated just west of the Seneto Gate, within the Malanja Depression.

NCAA

Visiting a MaasaiVillage

The Shifting Sand Dunes

The Shifting Sand Dunes are situated just 6km north-west of the Olduvai Gorge. Volcanic ash from the active volcano, Oldoinyo Lengai, accumulated on the plains to form dunes, some of which are stabilised, others not. The dunes north of the Olduvai Gorge are unstabilised dunes called 'barchans'. Barchans are crescent-shaped dunes formed as a result of the strong prevailing winds. In the case of the Shifting Sand Dunes, the strong north-westerly winds move the dunes an average of about 17m per year. They are about 9m high and about 100m along the curve (Hanby and Bygott, 1999).

The Shifting Sand Dunes

P L A C E S   T O   S E E

ARCHAEOLOGY

A R C H A E O L O G Y

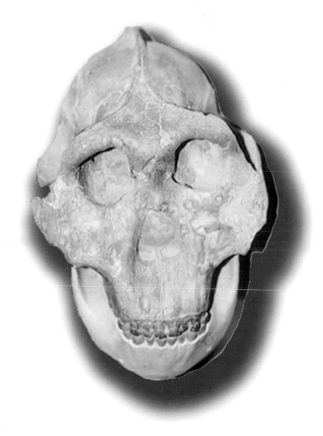

Nutcracker Man (Australopithecus boisei)

59

THE MAIN ARCHAEOLOGICAL SITES IN THE NCA ARE:

- **OLDUVAI GORGE**
  (2 million to 17 000 years ago)

- **LAETOLI**
  (3,6 to 2,8 million years ago)

- **NGORONGORO CRATER**
  (various proto-historic/more recent sites)

- **NASERA ROCK**
  (± 30 000 BC and more recent)

Archaeological sites - Olduvai Gorge

Olduvai Gorge

Wild Sisal (Sanseveria ehrenbergiana) or 'Oldupai'

ARCHAEOLOGY

Formation The floor of the Olduvai Gorge was formed about 2 million years ago when thick lava, consisting of basalt, from the Olmoti Volcano poured into the area. Subsequently, it was covered in layers of volcanic ash. A large saline lake was formed where the gorge is today. Faults caused tilting of the land, resulting in river action which carved out a gorge from the Lake Ndutu area to the Olbalbal Swamp (see 'Geology' on pg 72 for more details on the formation of the Olduvai Gorge). The formation of the gorge exposed the layers and the wealth of archaeological evidence within them.

Size of the gorge The gorge is about 50km long, stretching from Lake Ndutu to Olbalbal Depression, and 70m deep. In the immediate area of the main archaeological sites and the Olduvai Museum, it is up to 90m deep.

The Name The name was derived from 'Oldupai' which is the Maasai name for the Wild Sisal (*Sanseveria ehrenbergiana*) - a plant which is very abundant in the area.

Number of fossils The archaeological records cover about four million years, mainly from the Pleistocene era (see pg 68 for Geological Time Table). About 7 000 extinct animal species have been unearthed and there were about 60 different finds of hominid remains. The hominid remains date back from 2 million years to 17 000 years (see box on pg 62 for a description of the hominid discoveries in the area).

The Living Floor Another interesting site to visit is the 'Living Floor', about 5km east of the Museum where one can see tools and bones and remains from what was probably a shelter. To visit this site, one needs a guide from the centre.

Discovery of the Olduvai Gorge In 1911, Professor Wilhelm Kattwinkel, a German naturalist, stumbled upon some fossils whilst collecting butterflies in the Olduvai Gorge. He took the fossils for identification and they turned out to be from an extinct three-toed horse, belonging to the genus *Hipparion*. His report was followed up in 1913 by an expedition led by Professor Hans Reck, a German palaeontologist.

Louis and Mary Leakey The young Louis Leakey, a Kenyan-born pre-historian, saw the above specimens in the Berlin Museum. This prompted him to organise an expedition with Reck in 1931. He was later joined on this trip by his wife, Mary, and inspired by their finds, they established a camp there and devoted much of the rest of their lives to unravelling the secrets buried within the layers of the Olduvai Gorge. Louis Leakey died in 1972 but Mary Leakey continued her work and in 1976 discovered the Laetoli Footprints (see pg 65 for more details). She retired from field work in 1984 and died in 1996.

A photograph of the first expedition of Louis Leakey, as exhibited at the Olduvai Museum

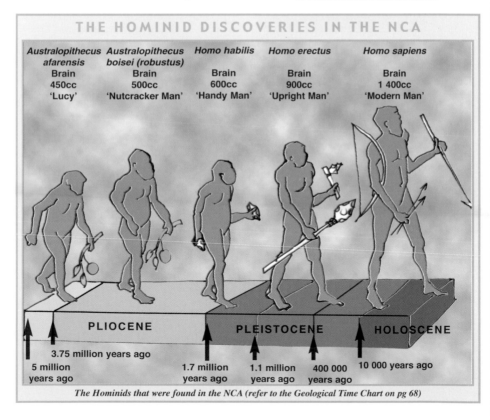

THE HOMINID DISCOVERIES IN THE NCA

Australopithecus afarensis	Australopithecus boisei (robustus)	Homo habilis	Homo erectus	Homo sapiens
Brain 450cc 'Lucy'	Brain 500cc 'Nutcracker Man'	Brain 600cc 'Handy Man'	Brain 900cc 'Upright Man'	Brain 1 400cc 'Modern Man'

PLIOCENE   PLEISTOCENE   HOLOSCENE

3.75 million years ago
5 million years ago
1.7 million years ago
1.1 million years ago
400 000 years ago
10 000 years ago

The Hominids that were found in the NCA (refer to the Geological Time Chart on pg 68)

ARCHAEOLOGY

THE HOMINID DISCOVERIES IN THE NCA CONTINUED

The discovery of 'Zinj' The finds at Olduvai from 1931 to 1959 were mainly of animal fossils and stone tools. The greatest find was a fairly complete Australopithene-type skull found by Mary Leakey on 17 July 1959. It was a robust skull which they named *Zinjanthropus boisei*, which means 'Boise's man from East Africa'. 'Zinj' is the Arabic name for East Africa and Charles Boise was the man who sponsored the expedition. Informally, it was referred to as 'Zinj' or 'Nutcracker Man'.

Zinj was one of the first hominid specimens to be carbon dated and a surprisingly ancient date of almost 1.8 million years was found. It was later named *Australopithecus boisei* and is also referred to as *A. robustus*. *A. boisei* was robust with a small brain (500cc) and was vegetarian. The remains were found in Beds I and II, close to the floor of the gorge. The site where Zinj was found is just a few minutes drive from the Olduvai Information Centre and it is possible to visit this historical site in the company of a guide.

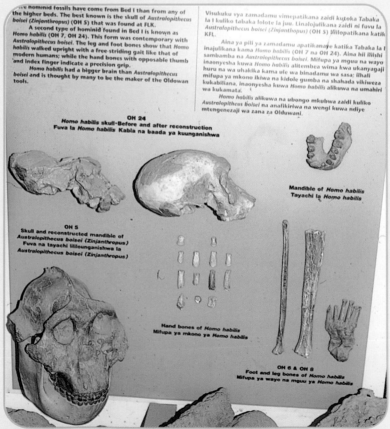

... hominid fossils have come from Bed I than from any of the higher beds. The best known is the skull of *Australopithecus boisei* (*Zinjanthropus*) (OH 5) that was found at FLK.

A second type of hominid found in Bed I is known as *Homo habilis* (OH 7, OH 24). This form was contemporary with *Australopithecus boisei*. The leg and foot bones show that *Homo habilis* walked upright with a free-striding gait like that of modern humans; while the hand bones with opposable thumb and index finger indicate a precision grip.

Homo habilis had a bigger brain than *Australopithecus boisei* and is thought by many to be the maker of the Oldowan tools.

Visukuku vya zamadamu vimepatikana zaidi kutoka Tabaka la I kuliko tabaka lolote la juu. Linalojulikana zaidi ni fuvu la *Australopithecus boisei* (*Zinjanthopus*) (OH 5) lililopatikana katik KFL.

Aina ya pili ya zamadamu apatikanaye katika Tabaka la I inajulikana kama *Homo habilis* (OH 7 na OH 24). Aina hii ililishi sambamba na *Australopithecus boisei*. Mifupa ya mguu na wayo inaonyesha kuwa *Homo habilis* alitembea wima kwa ukanyagaji huru na wa uhakika kama ule wa binadamu wa sasa; ilhali mifupa ya mkono ikiwa na kidole gumba na shahada vikiweza kukabiliana, inaonyesha kuwa *Homo habilis* alikuwa na umahiri wa kukamata.

Homo habilis alikuwa na ubongo mkubwa zaidi kuliko *Australopitheus boisei* na anafikiriwa na wengi kuwa ndiye mtengenezaji wa zana za Olduwani.

OH 24
Homo habilis skull-Before and after reconstruction
Fuva la *Homo habilis* Kabla na baada ya kuunganishwa

Mandible of *Homo habilis*
Tayachi la *Homo habilis*

OH 5
Skull and reconstructed mandible of
Australopithecus boisei (*Zinjanthropus*)
Fuva na tayachi lililounganishwa la
Australopithecus boisei (*Zinjanthropus*)

Hand bones of *Homo habilis*
Mifupa ya mkono ya *Homo habilis*

OH 6 & OH 8
Foot and leg bones of *Homo habilis*
Mifupa ya wayo na mguu ya *Homo habilis*

In the bottom left corner is a reconstruction of the skull of Australopithecus boisei and the other bones belong to the 'Handy Man' or Homo habilis, as exhibited at the Olduvai Museum. H. habilis occurred after A. boisei (Zinj) and was more advanced

Nutcracker Man or 'Zinj' (Australopithecus boisei)

Discovery of Homo habilis
It was at first suggested that Zinj had made the scrapers and tools found at Olduvai but it is now thought that it was 'Handy Man' or *Homo habilis*, whose fossil remains also occur at Olduvai. *Homo habilis* made tools and probably hunted small animals. It was smaller than Zinj but it had a slightly larger brain of 600cc. It disappeared about 1,5 million years ago.

Discovery of Australopithecus afarensis
It was found that both the above hominids were descendants of *Australopithecus afarensis*, the best fossil remains of which were recovered in Ethiopia in 1974. On Christmas Eve 1974, two archaeologists named Johansen and Gray found a piece of arm bone. After about three weeks of searching they found about two-fifths of a female skeleton of an ape-like human. In 1978 it was named *A. afarensis,* but informally it became famous as 'Lucy', named after the Beatles' song 'Lucy in the Sky with Diamonds' which was a favourite camp song at the time. The Laetoli Footprints were also found to have been made by *A. afarensis* (see pg 65 for details on the Laetoli Footprints). *A. afarensis* was strictly vegetarian and dates back at least 3,75 million years - more than one million years before the first stone tools appeared.

Discovery of Homo erectus
When Homo habilis disappeared about 1,5 million years ago, it made place for *Homo erectus* or 'Upright Man'. *Homo erectus* had a larger brain (900cc) and made better stone tools, such as axes. Evidence of *Homo erectus* was found in Bed IV at Olduvai Gorge.

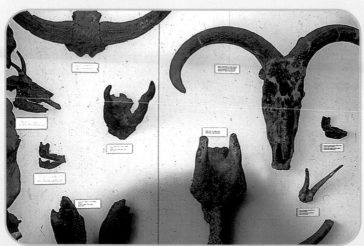

Some of the animals skulls found in the Olduvai Gorge, as exhibited at the Olduvai Museum

ARCHAEOLOGY

ARCHAEOLOGY

INTERPRETATION OF THE LAYERS OF OLDUVAI GORGE

The layers or beds of the Olduvai Gorge can be distinguished by the different colours of the soil

FLOOR OF THE GORGE

1,89 million years ago The Olmoti Volcano erupted and covered the area where the Olduvai Gorge is situated today. These eruptions formed the floor of the gorge and can be identified by the black basalts at the bottom. Before the formation of the Gorge, the lower beds consisted of a small, shallow, alkaline lake of about 5km by 10km. It attracted a menagerie of animals, some of which died inside or in the direct vicinity of the lake. Saline lakes provide the ideal conditions for fossilisation and many of the fossils were well preserved. As the animals died, their bones sank to the bottom of the lake into the mud. Here, a chemical process took place in which the calcium of the bones was replaced by silicon, a more durable compound, making it possible for us, today, to see evidence of early life on earth.

BED I AND LOWER BED II

More volcanic eruptions added layers and thus Bed I and the lower part of Bed II were formed. Two of the hominids found in these layers are *A. boisei*, also known as *A. robustus* or 'Nutcracker

Man' and *Homo habilis* or 'Handy Man'. **About 1,5 million years ago** The lake covering the current Olduvai area gradually emptied because the land was tilted through faulting. It resulted in a river running through the area, carving a shallow gorge, and the habitat was changed to riverine vegetation and open savanna. Lots of water accumulated, creating a favourable landscape and resulting in **gigantanism** - a phenomenon where species attained enormous sizes. Examples are the huge buffalo-like *Pelorovis* sp. which had down-curved horns and was much bigger than the present-day Buffalo. The Rhinoceros was twice its present size and a Pig was the size of a Hippopotamus. Evidence was also found of a sheep-like animal with huge horns of over 1,8m from tip to tip as well as a gigantic Giraffe, *Sivatherium* sp. with very large horns, and a Sabre-toothed Cat.

During the time of the earliest human toolmakers, an Elephant species called *Dinotherium,* roamed the area. Originally there were five families of Elephants and they all evolved from a common ancestor, *Moeritherium*, which was about the size of a Pig. *Dinotherium* had short tusks from the lower jaw, pointing downward. The tusks of modern Elephants originate in the upper jaw.

UPPER BED II

Although *A. boisei* was still around during this period, *Homo habilis* had disappeared to make place for *Homo erectus* or 'Upright Man'. *A. boisei* disappeared from the record soon afterwards - about 1,2 million years ago.

BED III

About 1,2 million years ago the area became drier, *A. boisei* disappeared and temporary salt lakes were formed. This era is represented by Bed III and can be identified by the red-brown colour of the soil. Very few fossils or tools were found in this layer.

BED IV

About 800 000 years ago Bed IV was formed and provides more evidence of 'Upright Man' *Homo erectus* and his sophisticated stone tools. *Homo erectus* disappeared at about 250 000 years ago to make place for *Homo sapiens*.

MASEK BEDS

About 600 000 to 400 000 years ago Keramasi, the eruptions of which formed the Masek beds, ceased to be active and

Oldoinyo Lengai, which is situated further north, became active. It remained so until the present, erupting at intervals. The last three times it erupted were in 1966, 1983 and 2006 (see pg 44 for more details on Oldoinyo Lengai). The 'Shifting Sand Dunes' at Olduvai Gorge are the result of dust eruptions from Oldoinyo Lengai.

NDUTU BEDS

About 100 000 to 30 000 years ago the Ndutu bed was formed and more faulting caused the formation of the Olbalbal Depression. Run-off from the plains caused the river to cut through Bed IV to Bed I, forming the gorge as we know it today.

NAISIUSIU BEDS

About 24 000 years ago the top bed, the Naisiusiu bed was formed.

Take note: It is difficult for the layman to distinguish the different beds, but the guide at the Museum will assist with this. The talk is mainly centred around this aspect.

Archaeological sites - Laetoli Footprints

An interpretation of early life on earth, as exhibited at the Olduvai Museum

ARCHAEOLOGY

ARCHAEOLOGY

Take note: This site is not open to tourists.

Louis Leakey died in 1972 but his wife, Mary, continued to make new discoveries. Her most exciting find after the death of her husband was the Laetoli Footprints in 1976, in an area called Laetoli, south of Olduvai Gorge and not too far north-west of Endulin.

A thorough study followed and it was established that the footprints were made during a time when the volcanoes were active. Volcanic ash, emitted from the nearby Sadiman Volcano, covered the plains and, when dampened by rain, provided a smooth surface on which tracks could be recorded. As soon as the tracks dried, a fresh layer of ash covered them, preserving them for millions of years.

The tracks were found to have been made by three hominids, probably two adults and a child. They were more ape-like than human and only ±1,3m tall. What distinguished them from other apes, is that they walked on two legs. It was found that the tracks were made by *Australopithecus afarensis* (the same species as 'Lucy', mentioned in the box on pg 63, which was discovered in Ethiopia). It had a brain size of 450cc - about one third of the modern human brain. Bone evidence of *A. afarensis* was also found at the Laetoli site. The Laetoli Footprints were dated at ±3.75 million years ago.

After the footprints were thoroughly studied and moulds were made, they were covered up again. It is not possible to visit the site but there is an excellent account of the discovery in the Olduvai Museum. There are also moulds of the original prints to be viewed in the museum.

Archaeological sites - Ngorongoro Crater

The Ngorongoro Crater has always attracted man. The Crater floor is extraordinarily rich in artifacts and proto-historic/more recent remains. However, all the finds remain unmarked and are not open to the public. There are many graves of varying origin, some of which are sacred. Many of the graves date back to the Stone-bowl People, but there are also more recent ones. Stone 'bau boards' were also found, which were used for a game similar to chess or drafts. There are also pottery remains, ancient cattle tracks and obsidian blades and barbs. Of more recent origin are the two farm ruins of the Seidentopf brothers, which date back to the turn of last century.

Archaeological sites - Nasera Rock

Nasera Rock was used during the Stone Age as a shelter. An abundance of bone material and artifacts has been recovered, some of which dates back to 30 000 BC. Please take care not to remove any material from this or any other archaeological site.

Nasera Rock

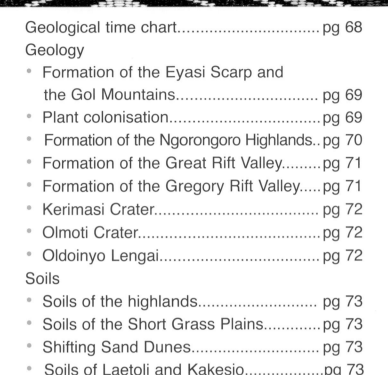

Oldoinyo Lengai - the only active volcano in the area

THE GEOLOGICAL TIME CHART

ERA	PERIOD	EPOCH	BEGAN (millions of years ago)	
CENOZOIC	QUARTERNARY *Homo sapiens* *Homo (sapiens) neanderthalensis* *Homo erectus*	Holocene	(10 000 years ago)	Modern Man
		Pleistocene	1,6 *Oldoinyo Lengai became active / formation of Olduvaai Gorge*	Stone-age Man
	TERTIARY *Homo habilis* *Australopithecus afarensis* *Australopithecus boisei*	Pliocene	5,3 *Slowing down of volcanic activity*	Mammals, Elephants, earliest hominids
		Miocene	23 *Formation of the Great Rift and Ngorongoro highlands*	Flowering plants Ancestral Dogs, Bears
		Oligocene	34	Ancestral Pigs, Apes
		Eocene	53	Ancestral Horses, Cattle, Elephants
		Palaeocene	65	Horses, Cattle, Elephants appear
MESOZOIC	CRETACEOUS		135	Extinction of dinosaurs mammals and flowering plants appear
	JURASSIC		205	Dinosaurs and ammonites abundant, birds and mammals appear
	TRIASSIC		250	Flying reptiles and dinosaurs
PALAEOZOIC	PERMIAN		300	Rise of reptiles and amphibians, conifers and beetles appear
	CARBONIFEROUS		355	First reptiles, winged insects
	DEVONIAN		410 *Formation of the 'Peneplains' and Kopjes*	First amphibians and ammonites, earliest trees and spiders
	SILURIAN		438	First spore-bearing land plants, earliest known coral reefs
	ORDOVICIAN		510	First fish-like vertebrates
	CAMBRIAN		570	Fossils first appear
PRECAMBRIAN			4 600 *Formation of the Eyasi Scarp and Gol Mountains*	Sponges, worms, algae, bacteria, oldest known traces of life

Geological Time Chart

GEOLOGY, SOILS AND HYDROLOGY

Geology

The following is a summarised description of the postulated geological processes that shaped the scenery as we know it today. For further reading, obtain a copy of the excellent publication 'Ngorongoro's Geological History' by Pickering (1993).

THE GEOLOGICAL TIMETABLE

The Precambrian and the Cambrian
The *Precambrian* era is the oldest geological era which represents about 4 000 000 000 (4 billion) years before the *Cambrian* era. The *Cambrian* geological era represents the first 60 million years of the *Palaeozoic* era, an era that started about 570 million years ago and which lasted for about 320 million years, ending with the *Permian* era. The underlying rocks of the NCA were mainly formed during the *Precambrian* era, in other words they are more than 570 million years old.

The Quarternary
The *Quaternary* is the most recent period of geological time and the *Pleistocene* denotes the first epoch of the *Quarternary*. This era is characterised by the evolution of man and is also the time when the Ngorongoro Highlands were formed. The volcanic activities resulted in layers and layers of volcanic tuft, which was deposited in the direction of the prevailing winds to form the endless plains west of the Ngorongoro Highlands.

MORE THAN 570 MILLION YEARS AGO

Formation of the Eyasi Scarp and the Gol Mountains
The Gol Mountains and Eyasi Scarp are some of the oldest formations in the NCA. It is difficult for geologists to say exactly how such old rocks were formed, but according to Pickering (1993), the picture is more or less as follows: More than 570 million years ago, during the *Precambrian* era, the entire region was covered by water, forming a huge sea into which sand and mud

were deposited. The weight caused the ocean floor to sag and more deposits accumulated. The first layers were compacted to form mudstones, sandstones and shales. The weight caused the rocks to become folded and some changed chemically. The sandstones folded and re-crystallised to form quartzite. The mudstones and shales were converted to quartz, feldspar, mica, hornblende, kianite and garnet. At the same time molten rock began to push its way up through the existing rock. The latter solidified to form granite. The shales and mudstones changed chemically and mixed with layers of granite to form gneisses. It is of interest to note here that the underlying rocks to the west of Seronera in the Serengeti, which were formed during the same era, are estimated to be ±2 500 million years old.

Uplifting of the land and subsiding of the ocean
Violent earth crust movements caused a weakness to develop near the boundary of the granites and the gneisses. These were ground into powder by earth movements. High temperatures caused the rock-powder to anneal and form a belt of flinty rocks. The ocean floor lifted and caused the ocean to subside. The uplifted land was changed by erosion caused by sun, water and wind. The rocks cracked as a result of continual heating and cooling, causing expansion and contraction. Thus, boulders and pebbles were formed which in turn were swept away by streams, creating valleys.

±400 MILLION YEARS AGO

Plant colonisation
About 400m years ago plants colonised the earth and soil was formed. Millions of years of erosion followed and eventually the ancient crystalline rock, which formed deep within the earth's crust, became exposed. A gently undulating plain or 'peneplain' was formed through further erosion. The kopjes so characteristic of the Serengeti Plain are the result of ancient quartzite and gneisses that proved more resistant to erosion (Pickering, 1993).

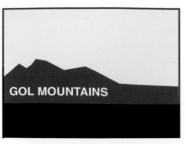

1. **More than 570 million years ago** The Gol Mountains were formed.

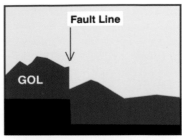

2. **20 million years ago** The Great Rift Valley was formed along a fault to the east of Gol.

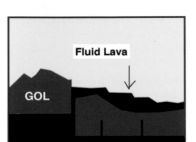

3. **20 to 15 million years ago** Fluid lava covered the area east of Gol right up to Kilimanjaro (250km away).

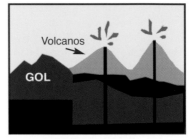

4. **15 to 2,5 million years ago** Vents were formed through which lava was pushed out to cause the build up of volcanic cones.

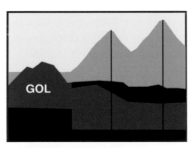

5. **2 million years ago** Slowing down of volcanic activity and formation of highlands completed. The Gregory Rift was formed and Keramasi Crater became active.

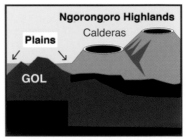

6. **600 000 to 370 000 years ago** Some craters collapsed to form calderas and subsequent erosion formed the landscape as we know it today. Oldoinyo Lengai became active and remains so.

Formation of the Ngorongoro Highlands

The Rift Valley as seen from Empakaai Rangers Post. One can see Keramasi Crater on the left of the photograph

±20 MILLION YEARS AGO

Formation of the Great Rift Valley A fracture occurred in the earth's crust along the western shore of what is now Lake Eyasi, through what later became Makarot Crater, up to the eastern side of the Gol Mountains. This forms part of the Great Rift Valley which is about 6 400km long and stretches from the Red Sea to the Kalahari Desert in Botswana. As mentioned previously, the Gol Mountains were formed long before that event - more than 500 million years ago. The land on the eastern side of Gol Mountains subsided about 1 000m to 1 800m relative to the land on the west.

Deposition of fluid lavas Elongated rifts were formed, through which fluid-basalt lavas oozed. The latter welled up from deep within the earth's crust and spread in waves as far east as Kilimanjaro.

±15 MILLION YEARS AGO

Formation of the Ngorongoro Highlands The elongated fissures eventually became sealed by the fluid-basalts, leaving only a few vents through which the lava continued to pour, resulting in the characteristic volcanic cones. The cones around each vent built up, expanded and merged to form the highlands. The original volcanoes were much higher than

they are today as many of them collapsed to form calderas, as was the case with the Ngorongoro, Olmoti and Empakaai Craters. The original estimated height of the Ngorongoro Crater was about 4 587m above sea-level. Today it is only 2 440m at its highest point. The famous Mount Kilimanjaro, which is about 250km east of the Ngorongoro Highlands, was formed in much the same way and during the same era, but it did not collapse to form a caldera. Kilimanjaro is the highest mountain in Africa at an amazing 5 895m above sea level.

15 to 2,5 MILLION YEARS AGO

Continued volcanic activity The building up of the highlands through volcanic activity continued for about 12,5 million years.

2,5 to 2 MILLION YEARS AGO

The Gregory Rift The second phase of faulting took place when another fracture occurred on the eastern side of the crater highlands, causing the land on the east to subside, forming what we know today as the Gregory Rift Valley. The wall of about 600m is evident when driving from Lake Manyara up to the highlands. Yet again, lava was forced out through vents during this phase and more volcanoes were formed.

GEOLOGY, SOILS AND HYDROLOGY

Kerimasi Crater The most prominent crater that was formed during the formation of the Gregory Rift is Keramasi. The latter was the source of vast amounts of soda ash that covered the Ngorongoro Highlands and the Serengeti Plains. Keramasi remained active until 600 000 to 400 000 years ago. During this period the Ngorongoro Crater took on its present form of a caldera.

±2 MILLION YEARS AGO

Slowing down of volcanic activity About 2 million years ago the main features of the area had been formed and general volcanic activity slowed down.

±1,89 MILLION YEARS AGO

Olmoti Crater About 1,89 million years ago Olmoti Volcano poured out thick lava flows consisting of dark, almost black basalts. This covered the area where the Olduvai Gorge is situated and forms the floor of the Gorge as we know it today. A shallow lake was formed in this area.

±1,5 MILLION YEARS AGO

Olduvai Gorge The lake emptied because the land was tilted through faulting. It resulted in the formation of a river which gradually carved out a shallow gorge. For the next ±100 million years layer upon layer of volcanic ash was deposited in the area, in fact, about 60m to 90m of it - the depth of the Olduvai Gorge today. During the process of deposition, evidence of

animal and human life was preserved within the layers (see pg 60 for details on the archaeological history of the area).

The layers of volcanic ash deposited in the Olduvaai Gorge can be distinguished by different colours

600 000 to 370 000 YEARS AGO

Oldoinyo Lengai During this time Keramasi ceased to be active and Oldoinyo Lengai, which is situated further north, became active, and remains so to this day. It is situated just north of the NCA on the valley floor. The elevation at the summit is 2878m above sea level and the elevation of the valley floor is ±1000m, making it about 1880m high. The first major eruption that was officially documented in 1917 and subsequent eruptions took place in 1926, 1940, 1966 and the most recent was in March 2006. Interestingly, Oldoinyo Lengai is the only volcano in the world that emits natrocarbonatite lava which is highly fluid and contains almost no silicon. It is almost black in colour or looks like brown foam, depending on how much gas is present. This kind of lava is much cooler than basaltic lavas, measuring about 510ºC (950ºF), compared to over 1100ºC (2000ºF) for basaltic lavas.

Oldoinyo Lengai

Geology continued

100 000 to 30 000 YEARS AGO

Olduvai Gorge More faulting caused the formation of the Olbalbal Depression and run-off from the plains caused the river to cut through all the layers or 'beds' of the Olduvai Gorge, forming the gorge as we know it today.

Shifting Sand Dunes Volcanic ash from Oldoinyo Lengai accumulated on the plains to form dunes, some of which are stabilised, others not. The 'Shifting Sand Dunes' north of the Olduvai Gorge are unstabilised, crescent-shaped dunes called 'barchans'. The dunes move an average of ±17m every year.

Soils of the NCA

The underlying rocks of most of the NCA are of volcanic origin, providing very fertile parent material for the formation of soils.

Soils of the highlands The soils on the eastern side of the highlands are the most fertile, consisting of basaltic lavas covered in brown tuff, which support montane forest. The woody vegetation provides excellent protection to the steep slopes. The porous nature of the volcanic soils is ideal for absorption, making the eastern highlands an important catchment area. The water appears as springs at the bottom of the Gregory Rift Valley. The rest of the highlands are covered in deep layers of volcanic ash, supporting a rich grass cover that protects the soil from erosion.

Elephants excavate and ingest the mineral rich soils of the highlands to supplement their diet

Soils of the Short Grass Plains The Short Grass Plains of Ndutu, Olduvai and the Sale Plains are also volcanic in origin. These soils are shallow as a result of their recent origin and they consist of calcareous (high mineral content) tuff covered by a shallow layer of volcanic dust. Volcanic soils are very alkaline and fertile. The calcareous tuff forms a hard

layer when it comes into contact with water, known as 'hard pan'. There are various layers of hard pan at different soil depths.

The hard pan retains water close to the surface and supports grasses very high in nutrition. The ability to retain surface water enables the grasses to germinate immediately after the first rains and to produce shoots shortly afterwards. Some of the grasses growing on the Short Grass Plains are dwarfed by the hard pan as they have the ability to grow much larger in other softer soil types. However, their high fertility and instant germination compensate for their small size. The nature of the soil thus has much to do with the fact that the migratory animals favour the Short Grass Plains during the rainy season (see the section on 'migration' on pg 105 for more details on the Short Grass Plains).

Dunes In the Sale area there are a number of dunes stabilised by vegetation. They consist of the black powder originating from the nearby active volcano, Oldoinyo Lengai. The Shifting Sand Dunes near Olduvai Gorge are good examples.

Soils of Laetoli and Kakesio In the Laetoli and Kakesio area, situated in the south-western section of the NCA, the soils consist of vertisols derived from calcareous tuff. These soils are less fertile than the soils of the eastern highlands and that of the Short Grass Plains, becoming extremely muddy and slippery during the rainy season.

GEOLOGY, SOILS AND HYDROLOGY

CATCHMENT AREAS

The Ngorongoro Crater The eastern side of the Ngorongoro Crater, mainly the area within the Ngorongoro Crater Forest Reserve, is an important catchment area for the valley below. Much of the drainage is underground as the porous volcanic soils in the highlands absorb the water which then reappears as springs at the foot of the escarpment. Some of the drainage is above ground, forming beautiful waterfalls in the highlands. The water eventually drains into basins within the valley - Lake Eyasi, Lake Manyara, Olmkoko and Lake Natron.

NCAA

A waterfall in the highlands

The Olmoti Crater The Olmoti Crater is of immense value for wildlife and cattle as a catchment area for rainwater. The floor of the crater acts as a filter to provide fresh water via the Munge River into the Mandusi Swamp. That water eventually drains into Lake Magadi where it becomes saline because of severe evaporation. The Olmoti Crater also provides water for the villages at the foot of the crater.

Oldeani Mountain The montane forest of Oldeani Mountain acts as a catchment area to provide water for humans and cattle from Endulen to the Ngorongoro Crater rim. It also supplies water to the areas west of Endulen,

together with Makarot. The streams one crosses while driving through the Lerai Forest in the Ngorongoro Crater originate on Oldeani Mountain, along with the Oldonyonoki River, which feeds the Gorigor Swamp.

Makarot Mountain Makarot is an important catchment area and provides water to the villages from Endulen further west. Some of the water west of Endulen also comes from the western side of Oldeani.

Lake Ndutu and Lake Masek These two lakes are part of the drainage system from west to east, where water from the Lake Ndutu area drains via the Olduvai Gorge into the Olbalbal Depression. Lake Ndutu (also called Lagarja) and Lake Masek form a shallow basin where the water accumulates from the nearby areas of slightly higher altitude. The water in both lakes is extremely saline but it attracts vast numbers of birds. Much of it evaporates during the dry season.

SPRINGS

The two most important springs in the Ngorongoro Crater are the Ngoitokitok Springs in the east and the Seneto Springs in the southwest. Both are formed by underground streams originating in the surrounding highlands.

BASINS

The basins within the NCA are the Mandusi Swamp and the Gorigor Swamp, both within the Ngorongoro Crater, as well as Lake Empakaai and Olbalbal, Embulbul and Malanja Depressions.

VEGETATION

Red Thorn Trees (Acacia lahai) on the slopes of the Ngorongoro Crater

VEGETATION

Take note: For each area the trees, shrubs, wild flowers and grasses will be discussed separately in sub-groups. Some interesting plant uses are also provided. The photographs are arranged alphabetically according to the scientific name. The four groups are:

1. Ngorongoro Crater rim and the ascent road (pg 77-82)

On the eastern rim of the Ngorongoro highlands the vegetation is very dense and lush, forming a thick forest. Although the rainfall is very high, it is not a rain forest as such, but a vegetation type called 'montane forest', consisting of giant trees that form an almost closed canopy. Because of the high rainfall, many of the trees are covered in ferns, mosses and lichens, the most common of the lichens belonging to the genus *Usnea*.

2. The descent road and floor of the Ngorongoro Crater (pg 83-86)

There is a dramatic difference in the vegetation of the rim and that of the descent road and the floor. The descent road is situated on the western side of the crater where the rainfall is much lower and the plant life is represented by dryland vegetation, for example, the Candelabra Trees (*Euphorbia* spp.) and trees with thorns, like *Acacias*. The floor of the crater consists mainly of grassland, wild flowers, swampy vegetation, Fever Tree woodland and isolated Fig Trees.

Elephants feeding on the lush grasses of the Ngorongoro Crater

3. Empakaai Crater rim (pg 87)

The vegetation is similar to that found along the Ngorongoro rim - lush montane forest with highland grassland. There is an overlap between the plant life found at both craters, but some species grow exclusively above 2 800m, occuring only at Empakaai.

4. Short Grass Plains, Olduvai Gorge and Lake Ndutu (pg 88-91)

The plant life of the Olduvai Gorge and of Lake Ndutu is situated in the 'rain shadow' of the highlands. This means that the clouds coming in from the east 'break' when they reach the highlands. The clouds that do manage to pass, often evaporate before they can supply rain, resulting in very dry conditions west of the highlands.

Therefore the plants growing in this area can be described as decidedly 'thorny' or 'spiny', *Acacia* and *Commiphora* Trees being dominant. In the Olduvai area *Sansevieria* and *Aloe* spp. are also very common - both genera being well adapted to survive in arid areas. The presence of thorns on plants is an adaptation to minimise evaporation from leaf surfaces and to deter browsing animals. The vegetation on the plains consists mainly of short grasses, small flowering herbs and a few scattered Umbrella Thorn Trees.

TREES

INTERESTING FACTS AND USES

TREES ON THE RIM

The **Red Thorns** (*Acacia lahai*) are flat-topped and grow closely together, forming a closed canopy. The name 'Red Thorn' refers to the red colour of the wood. This tree occurs only at high altitudes and is common on the Ngorongoro rim, near Seneto Gate in the south-west and near Lemala Gate in the north-east. The branches are covered in ferns, mosses and lichens. A bark infusion of this tree is taken orally to clean the bowels and it is also used to treat skin rashes. The active ingredient is the high levels of tannin. The wood is hard and useful for timber in construction work, bridge-building and it makes durable fence posts. The *Acacias* have nodules on their roots that have the ability to absorb nitrogen from the soil, thus recycling it.

This process is called 'nitrogen fixing'. The flat crown helps to break the force of raindrops, preventing soil erosion on the steep slopes.

Red Thorn Trees

The **Peacock Flower Tree** (*Albizia gummifera*) is rather flat-topped with a wide-spreading crown. The easiest way to recognise it is by the dark-green leaves which are glossy and compound, with large leaflets (12 pairs, each leaflet being 1cm to 2cm long). The leaflets are almost rectangular with one corner rounded and unequal sides. A root infusion is taken orally to treat tonsilitis. The flat crown helps to break the force of raindrops, preventing soil erosion. As with *Acacia* spp., nodules on

Peacock Flower Tree

the roots of *Albizia* trees also recycle or fix nitrogen, thus ultimately enriching the soil.

The easiest tree to identify on the crater rim is the **Pillarwood** *(Cassipourea malosana)* which can be recognised by its tall, straight stem (up to 40m) and relatively small canopy. The bark has breathing pores arranged in horizontal lines. The wood is very strong and elastic and was once used for poles in heavy construction.

Pillarwood

The **Broad-leaved Croton** *(Croton macrostachyus)* has a wide, spreading canopy, a pale grey trunk of up to 25m tall and large, heart-shaped leaves which are slightly silver underneath. The leaves turn orange at maturity. The fruits are pea-sized and clustered together to form pendulous spikes. The wood is used for making small objects such as stools and axe handles but like many other *Croton* spp., it has many medicinal uses as well. A root infusion is taken orally to treat stomach worms. The smoke from the burnt leaves is inhaled to treat coughs. A root extraction is taken for malaria and venereal disease and the leaf juice is said to improve blood clotting, making it an important treatment for bleeding wounds. The bark from the roots and twigs can be used to cure skin rashes (Dharani, 2002).

Broaded-leaved Croton

VEGETATION

The **Strangler Fig** (*Ficus thonningii*) can be recognised by the red-tipped aerial roots that hang from the upper branches. The seeds germinate in the fork of a host tree, after which it sends down aerial roots. When reaching the ground, the aerial roots thicken and twine around the host tree, eventually killing it - hence the common name of 'Strangler Fig'. It is not a parasite in the true sense of the word as it does not obtain nutrients from the host, but it uses the host as support. The Maasai name of this tree is 'Oretiti'. Traditionally, the Strangler Fig serves as an important meeting place for tribal members and is regarded as the sacred home of ancestral spirits. In the crater, as one drives from the descending road to the Lerai Forest, there is a beautiful group of Strangler Figs on the left. This group of trees is called Tatogaa Ritual Site and is used for religious purposes by the Maasai who regard it as sacred. The big tree on the lawn at Simba A Camp Site is a Strangler Fig and just west of Ngorongoro Crater Lodge is another magnificent specimen.

Strangler Fig

The bark fibre can be used to make strings and the branches have soft wood - ideal for producing fire by friction. If the root is pounded, an adhesive juice can be obtained. This was used in the past to trap birds and hares. Because Fig Trees do not have conventional flowers (the flowers form within the fig itself), pollination takes place inside the figs. This is effected by a small parasitic wasp that enters the fig to lay its eggs. The larvae of the Fig Tree Blue Butterfly (*Myrina silenus ficedula*) feeds on the young leaves of this tree.

The **Nuxia** *(Nuxia congesta)* is another common tree along the rim, and has a distinctly fluted trunk. The trees are seen on the road to Ngorongoro Wildlife Lodge and on the road to the NCA headquarters. The flowers are borne in profuse, congested heads - hence the specific name 'congesta'. The wood is soft and white and used only as kindling.

Nuxia

TREES ON THE ASCENT ROAD

The pink flowered **Cape Chestnut** (*Calodendrum capense*) is very noticeable on the ascent road and on the rim when in flower, as the whole tree turns pink. The fruit is ±5cm across, five-lobed and very knobbly and spiny. The leaves are dark, regularly veined and ±14cm long. This is a common garden tree. The wood is pliable and used for house building, stools and knife handles.

Cape Chestnut

Near the stream that one crosses about halfway up the ascent road, one can see the magnificent **Steudner's Dracaena (*Dracaena steudneri*)** which has sword-like leaves radiating from a central point, and which can grow up to 15m high. It is common in high rainfall forest areas, favouring the valleys because of its preference for moist soil. The flowers are borne on one metre long flowerheads and they open at night with a sharp, sweet smell, dying the next day. Although it prefers wet soil, the tree is drought resistant, grows easily from cuttings and is often used in gardens (Noad and Birnie, 1992).

Steudner's Dracaena (Dracaena steudneri)

VEGETATION

The **Wild Banana** (*Ensete ventricosum*) is the indigenous representative of the Banana Tree. It grows to about 12m high, almost exclusively in upland forest valleys. It can be distinguished from the common tropical Banana Tree by the pendulous flowerheads up to 3m long. It yields a valuable fibre. This tree is very low in vitamin A, an essential vitamin for proper eyesight development. This can lead to blindness in areas such as Ethiopia, where the Wild Banana is used as a staple food. However, in Ethiopia as well as other developing countries, cataracts and *Trachoma* are the main causes of blindness.

Trachoma is a sexually transmitted disease caused by a parasite, *Chlamydia trachomatis*, which infects mucous membrane surfaces. This disease also causes the eye-lashes to turn inward, scarring the eye surface and causing extreme pain for the patient. *Trachoma* is often transmitted from mother to child during childbirth.

Wild Banana

SHRUBS

INTERESTING FACTS AND USES

Buddleia (*Buddleia polystachya*) has sharp smelling, orangy-yellow flowers arranged in spikes. The macerated branches of this plant, mixed with water, produce a froth and they are commonly used to scour cooking pots. The dried twigs are used for starting fire by friction and are also very effective as kindling.

Buddleia
(*Buddleia polystachya*)

The **Giant St. John's Wort** (*Hypericum revolutum*) can be recognised by its small leaves. It has a curry-like odour when crushed and is said to contain Hypericum, a chemical that causes photosynthesization in sheep. This is when the unpigmented area in the face develops sores when it comes into contact with the sun.

Giant St. John's Wort
(*Hypericum revolutum*)

The **Crotalaria** (*Crotalaria agatiflora*) is very common on the rim and can be recognised by its yellow, pea-like flowers borne towards the top of the plant on erect branches, with three leaflets. A root extraction is used to treat gonorrhoea but taken in large quantities, it may damage the liver.

Crotalaria
(*Crotalaria agatiflora*)

The purple-flowered **Giant Vernonia** (*Vernonia auriculifera*) is also very common and easy to recognise by its large leaves and purple composite flowers. It belongs to the Daisy family (*Compositae*). The leaves and root are used to prepare a poultice to treat external wounds.

Giant Vernonia
(*Vernonia auriculifera*)

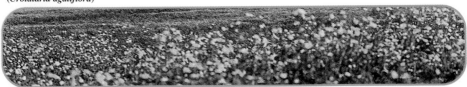

Aspilia mossambicensis on the crater rim

V E G E T A T I O N

WILD FLOWERS

INTERESTING FACTS AND USES

VEGETATION

Take note: The flowers that occur on the rim and the ascent road of the Ngorongoro Crater, may also be seen at Empakaai.

The wild flowers, herbs and climbers along the rim are numerous and varied, but yellow is definitely the dominant colour. Look out for the climber, the Golden Shower (*Senecio hadiensis*), which climbs over trees and is very dominant in places. Other common yellow-flowered species belonging to the Daisy family are *Helichrysim odoratissimum, Conyza newii, Crassocephalum montuosum, Crassocephalum vitellinum* and *Aspilia mossambicensis*. The yellow-flowered *Verbascum brevipedicellatum*, belonging to the Fox glove family *(Scrophulariaceae)* is also common along the rim.

Commelina benguallensis

with water, it is used to bathe sore eyes. The plant juice is said to be an astringent, thus stopping blood flow in external wounds. It is also used to treat diarrhoea and dysentry.

Senecio hadiense

Crassocephalum montuosum

Aspilia mossambicensis

Conyza newii

The **Flame Lily** (*Gloriosa superba*) is a striking plant with five upward curving, red and yellow petals, resembling flames. It is extremely poisonous, the rootstock more so than the leaves and flowers. Yet, porcupines eat the corm with apparent impunity. The powdered corm is used all over Africa as an aphrodisiac. It is also administered to infertile women. However, studies have confirmed that administration to pregnant women can result in deformed babies. The plant contains the highly toxic alkaloid, colchicine, a well-known product used in the treatment of gouty arthritis. The corm is used externally as a disinfectant to treat wounds, haemorrhoids, skin diseases and toothache. A root infusion is taken against worms. A sap derived from the root is used as a poison to control pests such as rodents, and a small quantity is potent enough to kill a dog.

The flame lily

The corm of this plant takes on a peculiar, gnarled shape and it is often used in fertility rites where a child of a certain gender is preferred. In Kwazulu-Natal in South Africa, a mother is given an infusion made from the corm that resembles the genitals of the required gender but, as was pointed out above, this often leads to misformed babies.

Mucilage (a slimy substance) from the flowering parts of the **Blue Wandering Jew** (***Commelina benguallensis***) is used to treat thrush in infants. Bruised leaves are applied to external wounds and burns. The plant juice is taken orally to ease sore throats and mixed

Gloriosa superba

The succulent **Kalanchoe** or **Snuff Plant** (*Kalanchoe lanceolata*) is an erect plant with attractive orange flowers and paired, boat-shaped, succulent leaves. The dried, ground plant is mixed with snuff. When snuffed, it

causes severe sneezing which is said to clear the head in the case of a cold. The powdered root is applied to the nose during colds to preventy cold sores.

Kalanchoe lanceolata

The **Smelly Cucumber** (*Momordica foetida*) is a climber with a woody rootstock. The leaves are simple (mostly heart-shaped) or divided with serrated edges. The flowers are cream-coloured and the plant has an unpleasant smell when crushed. The root and leaf are used to treat earache and roundworm. The plant is also used as a laxative, or to induce

vomiting and abortion. In Tanzania the fruit pulp is considered poisonous to weevils, moths and ants and it is commonly used as an insect repellent.

Momordica foetida

The **Pink Pavonia** (*Pavonia urens*) is one of

the most attractive plants along the rim with its delicate pink flowers, dark pink centres and long styles. Strong ropes can be made from the stems.

Pavonia urens

The **Tattoo Plant** (*Plumbago zeylanica*) is a perennial climber with white, tubular flowers with a green calyx covered in sticky hairs. It is said that by tying the fresh root closely to the skin and leaving it for 24 hours, a blister will form and after the skin is removed, the skin will darken. It is widely used in Africa for cosmetic tattooing. The root contains 4% plumbagin, a chemical that stimulates smooth muscles and the central nervous system. Thus, root scrapings pushed into the uterus, cause the muscles of the uterus wall to contract, which can result in abortion. This plant also dilates peripheral blood vessels, causing the lowering of blood pressure, but large doses can result in paralysis. An extraction of the root is used to treat hookworm in cattle, scabies, skin infections and yaws. The root juice is

applied externally to the penis as a very painful treatment for sexual diseases. The plant juice is applied directly to infected eyes of cattle and the bruised root is fed to livestock to bring on ovulation.

Plumbago zeylanica

The **Larkspur** (*Delphinium leroyi*) is related to the highly poisonous *Delphinium ajacis,* which has caused severe stock losses in Europe and America. However, no toxicity has thus far been reported for this plant.

Delphinium leroyi

The **Khaki Weed** (*Tagetes minuta*) was introduced during World War I in horse fodder by the British, referred to by the Boers in South Africa as the 'Khakis' because of the colour of their uniform - hence the common name.

British soldier 'Khaki'

Khaki Weed (Tagetes minuta)

V E G E T A T I O N

81

VEGETATION

GRASSES

INTERESTING FACTS AND USES

The most common grass species along the rim road is the **Highland Tussock Grass** (***Eleusine jaegeri***), which grows in disturbed areas and forms large, homogeneous stands.

It is very tough and robust and is ignored by grazing animals. It has an important function in soil binding as it has a strong rhizome system. It tends to take over in highland grassland.

Highland Tussock Grass
(*Eleusine jaegeri*),

Also common but a little more palatable is ***Pennisetum sphacelatum,*** a grass with a spiky inflorescence that also grows in tussocks. It becomes very unpalatable when mature but has an important function in soil binding.

Pennisetum sphacelatum

Couch Grass (*Cynodon dactylon*) has a digitate (finger-like) flowerhead and grows ±30cm high. It is an indicator of saline soils and tends to take over when mild over-grazing occurs. It has a vigorous rhizome system which enables it to form large stands and which makes it very effective in erosion control. It is not as high in nutrition as *Themeda triandra* but it has a very high yield. The more it is grazed, the more it grows, making it ideal as a lawn grass. An extraction of the rhizome is used as a blood purifier, to cause urination and to bring down swelling. It is also effective against heartburn and to treat external wounds. When this grass wilts, it can cause bloat in animals because of the large concentration of prussic acid that builds up in the stomach. The rhizomes are favoured by Spring Hares.

Couch Grass
(*Cynodon dactylon*)

Tussock grasses on the highlands

TREES

INTERESTING FACTS AND USES

An *Acacia* that immediately catches the eye inside the crater is the yellow-barked **Fever Tree (*Acacia xanthophloea*)** which forms large stands in the crater, the most noticeable of which is the Lerai Forest. 'Lerai' is the Maasai name for the tree. It is called the Fever Tree because in the early days it was suspected of causing malaria. The truth is that it grows in the same areas that mosquitoes frequent - along permanent water courses - the female mosquito being the carrier of the malaria parasite, *Trypanosoma* sp.

Fever Tree forest in the Ngorongoro Crater

The **Candelabra (*Euphorbia candelabrum*)** is a succulent tree that is very easy to recognise by its thick (±20cm), succulent, upward-pointing branches. The branches are four-winged, constricted at intervals, green and have small, paired spines on the edges. The tree occurs mainly on kopjes but also in woodlands, near or on termite mounds and in thorn bushland. The flowers are yellowish, fleshy and produced

in groups above the paired spines. Interestingly, bees favour this tree but the honey produced cannot be eaten by man as it burns the mouth.

Euphorpia candelabrum

The fruit is a green, pea-sized capsule. The white latex of this tree is very poisonous and can cause blindness. Like all succulents, it has the ability to survive severe droughts because it uses its stems as storage organs. This plant is known as 'Mkalamu' in Swahili and is used in Tanzania to treat post-natal ailments. In large quantities, it is used to induce abortion but the wrong dosage can result in death. The Iraqw tribe has a severe treatment for piles and worms - a branch is stripped of its thorns and bark and inserted into the rectum (Martin, 2000).

The **Tree Euphorbia (*Euphorbia bussei*)** is similar to the above species but the stems are more divided and form bunches at the top of the branches. The uses and poisonous properties are similar to that of *E. candelabrum*.

Euphorbia bussei

The **Quinine Tree (*Rauvolfia caffra*)** is an attractive evergreen tree that one can see along the streams in the Lerai Forest. It has yellowish-brown, corky bark and whorls of three to five shiny, leathery leaves. All parts of the tree exude a toxic milky latex, but a bark infusion is nevertheless used as a powerful medicine to disinfect external wounds and to treat coughs. Because of its potency, it is very effective in killing maggots in external wounds.

Rauvolfia caffra

WILD FLOWERS

INTERESTING FACTS AND USES

VEGETATION

The most common wild flowers on the floor of the crater are the purple coloured *Gutenbergia cordifolia* and the yellow-coloured *Aspilia mossambisencis*, *Bidens schimperi* and *Bidens taitensis*.

The **Milkweed (*Asclepias fruticosa*)** is easily recognised by its sharply-pointed fruit covered in purplish bristles. The plant is toxic in large quantities but infusions of all plant parts are effective against stomach complaints, diarrhoea and coughs. It irritates the intestinal wall and stimulates intestinal movement. It is a good substitute for Senna (a yellow-flowered tropical plant of which the pods are used as a laxative). The latex of the Milkweed is used to remove warts. The bark is very strong and can be used as string. The crushed plant is stuffed into mole holes to deter them and the silky seed threads are used to stuff mattresses. The seed threads are high in cellulose content (82%), making it very effective as tinder as it causes an instant energy release when lit. This property was well explored by early European settlers.

They used it in tinderbox lamps and as a substitute for guncotton where it was mixed with gunpowder to load cartridges.

Milkweed fruits

The African Monarch Butterfly (*Danaus chrysippus*) is closely associated with this plant as the larvae feed on it. The butterfly and larvae are thus poisonous and ignored by most insect predators.

Male

Common Diadem Butterfly   *African Monarch Butterfly*

Many butterflies that are not poisonous, such as the female of the Common Diadem (*Hypolimnas misippus*), mimic the Monarch to prevent predation. The male Common Diadem looks like a different species of butterfly, being black with large, blue-edged spots. The Milkweed is very similar to the closely related *Gomphocarpus physocarpus,* the fruits of the latter being more rounded, lacking the sharp point, but they are also covered in purplish bristles.

The **Sodom Apple (*Solanum incanum*)** belongs to a genus that has mauve, star-shaped flowers with yellow stamens in the middle, arranged like a pyramid. This is an erect, unfriendly weed covered in velvety hairs and with prickles scattered all along the stems and stalks. An extraction of the root is taken orally for chest complaints and haemorrhoids. The fruit is poisonous when green but is administered orally and externally to animals to treat ringworm, a skin disease caused by a fungus. The root is chewed for toothache, to treat stomach pains and for indigestion.

Sodom Apple

Bushmen's Tea or **Fever Bush (*Lippia javanica*)** is commercially marketed in Botswana as a herbal tea. Not only is it a refreshing drink, but it also has medicinal properties, being used for coughs, colds, bronchial ailments and fever. It is used as an eye-wash for sore eyes, and the smoke from the burnt leaves is used to clear the chest. The leaves are highly aromatic and when burnt, are effective as an insect repellent.

Fever Bush

The **Lion's Paw** (*Leonotis nepetifolia*) is an erect, down-covered plant with paired, drooping leaves borne below the globose flowerheads that occur at intervals along the stem. The flowers are orange-red and tubular. The dried leaves are smoked in southern Africa but it does not have any hallucinogenic properties as is implied by its one common name 'Wild dagga'. 'Dagga' is the southern African name for marijuana. A decoction of the plant, mixed with salpetre, is used to treat syphilitic ulcers and mixed with pumpkin seeds, it is taken orally against tapeworm. This species occurs at lower altitudes on the plains but also occur on the highlands up to 2 000m.

Lion's Paw

GRASSES

INTERESTING FACTS AND USES

The main grass species that occurs in the open areas in the crater is **Oats Grass** (*Themeda triandra*). This is one of the most common grazing grasses in Tanzania. It grows on all soil types and has an average to high nutritive value. It occurs in tall grass areas within the crater and is easy to recognise by the characteristic oat-like spikelets and the fact that the grass turns reddish-brown at maturity. It is extremely variable in habitat choice, growing in lowlands as well as in mountain grassland. Its presence is an indication of healthy, well-managed, climax veld where it forms large uniform communities (consisting of only one kind of plant).

Themeda triandra

One of the main grass species in the swampy areas is the rusty-coloured **Rhodes Grass** (*Chloris gayana*). It prefers well-drained, moist soils and it is an indicator of stable conditions. It can be recognised by the digitate (finger-like) flowerheads with their red-brown colour. Rhodes Grass is a highly valued forage grass and various strains are being cultivated worldwide. It is also very effective in erosion control, especially in damp

Chloris gayana

Hyparrhenia rufa

areas such as dam walls. The grass was named after Cecil John Rhodes (1853-1902), the British colonial prime minister of South Africa who introduced the grass to South Africa in 1895 from India, for its high nutritious value.

Thatching Grass (*Hyparrhenia rufa*) can be seen near the swampy areas in the crater. It has rusty-brown, paired racemes (spikes) and grows up to 2,5m high. It is a valuable fodder grass early in the rainy season but as soon as it becomes woody, it is ignored. It is commonly used as a thatching grass. It prefers moist soil types and is an indicator of under-utilisation where it tends to form climax communities (a stage in the development of a plant community during which it remains stable under the prevailing environmental conditions).

VEGETATION

Odyssea sp.

Around the pans, the most saline resistant of all grass species is **Odyssea** sp., probably *O. paucinervis,* which grows closest to the pans. It grows from rhizomes and is important in erosion control around salty pans.

Another very saline resistant species is **Spike Grass,** or **Spiky Dropseed (Sporobolus spicatus)**, which grows around salt lakes. It is called 'dropseed' because the seeds are dropped to the ground at maturity. It can be recognised by its narrow spikes. The leaves are rigid and spiky - a very unfriendly grass. It is totally unpalatable but it is a good indicator of saline soils and a handy soil binder around salt lakes where it forms climax communities.

Sporobolus spicatus

Cynodon dactylon

Couch Grass (Cynodon dactylon) has a digitate (finger-like) flowerhead and grows ±30cm high. It is an indicator of saline soils and tends to take over when mild overgrazing occurs. It has a vigorous rhizome system which enables it to form large stands and which makes it very effective in erosion control. It is not as high in nutrition as *Themeda triandra* but it has a very high yield. The more it is grazed, the more it grows, making it ideal as a lawn grass. An extraction of the rhizome is used as a blood purifier, to cause urination and to bring down swelling. It is also effective against heartburn and to treat external wounds. When this grass wilts, it can cause bloat in animals because of the large concentration of prussic acid that builds up in the stomach. The larva of the common Evening Brown Butterfly (*Melanitis leda*) feeds on this species. The rhizomes are favoured by Spring Hares.

Grazers such as Zebra are attracted by the nutritious grasses inside the crater

VEGETATION

Empakaai Crater - Trees & Wild flowers

TREES

INTERESTING FACTS AND USES

Hygenia (*Hygenia abyssinica*) is one of the most prominent trees as one approaches the  Empakaai Crater wall. It occurs almost exclusively above 3 000m and is therefore absent along the Ngorogoro Crater wall, which is only 2 440m at its highest point. It has drooping, feathery leaves and the flowers

Hygenia

form masses of bright pink to red drooping clusters, borne mainly at the top. The female flowers are brighter in colour than the male flowers. The wood is hard and dark-red, often used for carpentry. A bark infusion is a well-known traditional medicine and is said to be a very effective cure for diarrhoea. In stronger concentrations it can even induce abortion. An infusion of the female flower-heads is said to be a potent medicine against tapeworms (Dharani, 2002).

WILD FLOWERS

INTERESTING FACTS AND USES

Take note: Many of the flowers that occur on the rim of the Ngorongoro Crater also occur at Empakaai. However, some occur only above 3 000m, and are thus only found at Empakaai.

The **Parrot Beak Gladiolus (*Gladiolus dalenii,*** formerly known as *G. natalensis*)  is a very attractive plant with bright orange flowers, resembling a parrot's beak. It belongs to the Iridaceae family and looks very similar to the garden Gladiolus (*G. primulinus*). It occurs in grassland 1 200m to 3 000m above sea level. In South Africa various *Gladiolus* spp. are used to treat dysentery and diarrhoea. Extractions of the corm are used to treat infertile women and the

Gladiolus

smoke from the burning corm is inhaled as a cure for colds. The plant has been found to contain saponin, a substance that froths when mixed with water and it is successfully used as a disinfectant. It is also used to treat stomach troubles and as an emetic (to cause vomiting).

The **Red Hot Poker (*Kniphofia thomsonii*)** is very common at Empakaai. It grows from a rhizome and may form clusters or occur solitary. The vein endings of the leaves are rich in tannin.

Red Hot Poker

The **Woolly Lion's Paw (*Leonotis mollissima*)** is very similar to *L. nepetifolia* but the leaves are woolly, ovate, heart-shaped and not paired below each flowerhead as is the case in *L. nepetifolia*. Both species occur on the highlands. The flowers are in one to three terminal, spherical masses. This species occurs above 2 000m and is the most likely to be seen in the highlands. As one approaches Empakaai Crater, one passes through a long stretch of *Leonotis*, which attract a variety of sunbirds, most noticeably the Malachite Sunbird with its long tail. The leaf is used as a snake-bite remedy and the root is used to treat external sores. Experiments have shown that if eaten in large quantities, it will cause gastroenteritis, but in small quantities is effective against intestinal cramps, dysentry and indigestion.

Woolly Lion's Paw

TREES

INTERESTING FACTS AND USES

VEGETATION

OLDUVAI GORGE AND LAKE NDUTU

The Olduvai Gorge, Lake Ndutu and the Short Grass Plains are all situated in the 'rain shadow' of the highlands, where the rainfall is much lower. The most common trees in these areas are the *Acacia* spp., the *Commiphora* spp., the Wild Caper Bush (*Capparis tomentosa*) and the Sickle Bush (*Dichrostachyus cinerea*). All the above trees have thorns, a typical adaptation of trees growing in dry areas which helps to minimise waterloss and to deter browsing animals.

The **Umbrella Thorn (*Acacia tortilis*)** has a characteristic flattened, umbrella-shaped canopy. The flowers are cream-coloured balls and the pods are twisted spirally. It is widespread in open savannahs, along slopes, on hillsides and near rivers. It is very common at Lake Ndutu. The bark is used for tanning and for dyes. It prefers clayey soils but is often associated with kopjes. It is the only tree that can penetrate the hard pan (solidification of the soil) of the Short Grass Plains. It is a very nutritious tree, the leaves, flowers and pods being sought after by browsing animals and primates. Elephants show a special preference for the bark of this tree, often destroying them in the process of de-barking.

Umbrella Thorn (Acacia tortilis)

The **Black Thorn (*Acacia mellifera*)** is closely associated with disturbed, over-grazed soils, bared by sheet and gully erosion. It is an invader and spreads very rapidly. It loses all its leaves in winter but bursts into masses of cream-coloured flowers in spring. The thorns are very nasty - short, strong, curved and needle-sharp. A strong root infusion is used for stomach troubles, syphilis and as an aphrodisiac. The wood ash is an effective hair straightener and dye, imparting a brick-red colour to black hair. The heart-wood is dark, almost black - hence the common name. The wood is termite and borer proof and slightly elastic - excellent for axe handles. It exudes a good quality gum. One can often see nests of Communal Spiders *(Stegodyphes sp.)* in this tree and in other *Acacias*.

Black Thorn (Acacia mellifera)

The **Wild Caper Bush (*Capparis tomentosa*)** can be a shrub or a tree (up to 7m) but it often climbs over other plants. It is dull, grey-green in colour and has strong, paired, curved thorns all along the stem. The bark is grey but the branchlets are covered in yellowish hairs (hence the specific name '*tomentosa*', which means 'hairy'). The flowers are large and showy (±3,5cm), consisting of a mass of stamens of the same length. The fruits are ±3,5cm in diameter, round with a stout stalk, green, turning pinky-orange. The plant is considered poisonous but it is eaten by animals and used medicinally. The root bark is used as a laxative.

The decorticated root (core removed) is chewed to cure coughs. The ashed root, mixed with animal fat, is used to treat sensitive teats in cows. It is also used to treat piles by placing a strong root extraction in a hot bath and having the patient sit in it for 2 hours.

Wild Caper Bush
(Capparis tomentosa)

The astringent action is said to contract blood vessels and to prevent bleeding. The larvae of two common butterflies, the Brown-veined White (*Belenois aurota aurota*) and the Queen Purple Tip (*Colotis regina*), feed on this plant.

The **Sickle Bush** (*Dichrosthys cinerea*) is a small (3m to 5m), untidy, multi-stemmed Acacia-like bush and is often associated with kopjes. It can be recognised by the woody spines which are the cause of many a flat tyre. The leaves are fine and feathery and the flowers are spectacular - cylindrical spikes with a pink sterile section and a thicker, yellow, fertile section. The flowers are commonly referred to as 'Chinese Lanterns'. The pods are borne in twisted, roundish clusters and are favoured by all browsers. The wood is very hard and termite-resistant, suitable for tool handles. This tree is very high in nutritional value but tends to take over in disturbed areas - it is thus an encroacher. Extractions of this plant are a widely used cure for snake and insect bites. The leaves are chewed to treat toothache and the macerated leaves are applied to external wounds. Leaf extracts are used to treat stomach troubles and diarrhoea and when mixed with salt, can be used as an eye-wash. The larvae of the Topaz Blue Butterfly (*Azanus jesous jesous*) feed on the flowers and buds.

Sickle Bush Flowers
(Dichrostachys cinerea)

Commiphora (*Commiphora trothae*) is the most common Commiphora in the Serengeti National Park, especially in the south. Members of this genus can be identified by their flaky, papery bark. This small tree (2m to 5m) is mostly associated with *Acacia* Trees. It prefers well-drained soils of ridges and slopes, especially soils derived from granites and gneisses. The bark is grey-green, peeling in orangey scrolls and the tree has a gnarled knoll. The stems are spine-tipped. The leaves are trifoliate with the terminal leaflet being longer than the side ones, and the leaf margins are serrated. It is very similar to *C. africana* which occurs mainly north of the Bololedi River in the Lobo area of the Serengeti. *C. africana* also occurs in the Kalahari Desert in Botswana where the San (Bushmen) use the body juice of a larva (*Diamphidia simplex*) that feeds on the roots as a lethal arrow poison.

Commiphora
(Commiphora trothae)

THE PLAINS

There are no trees on the plains except near the rivers and rocky outcrops. The main reason for this is that the roots of the saplings cannot penetrate the 'hard pan', a hard layer that is a few centimetres under the soil surface. This hard layer is the result of the rise and fall of the moisture levels of the lime-rich soil.

A tree that has the ability to penetrate the hard pan is the **Umbrella Thorn** (*Acacia tortilis*), which is described on pg 97. Along the rivers and near kopjes one may see the latter in association with the **Fever Tree** (*Acacia xanthophloea*). of which a description is provided on pg 89.

Umbrella Thorn
(Acacia tortilis)

WILD FLOWERS

INTERESTING FACTS AND USES

Aloe secundiflora

Aloe secundiflora is a middle-sized aloe with numerous flowerheads. The leaf sap is used as a laxative and for skin healing, burns and ulcers.

Aloe volkensii is a tall aloe, up to 6m. It has a terminal rosette of grey-green, succulent leaves and much-branched panicles of red-orange

flowers. It grows in rocky bushland, kopjes and hills and it is especially common at Olduvai Gorge and on kopjes and hills in the Serengeti. The leaf sap is used as a laxative and for skin healing, burns and ulcers. Aloe flowers are a favourite with sunbirds.

Aloe volkensii

The **Climbing Cactus,** also known as the **Edible-stemmed Vine** or **Four-angled Vine** (**Cissus quadrangularis**) occurs commonly on the kopjes and has edible stems. The fresh leaves and powdered stems are applied to burns and wounds and is said to be an effective treatment for saddle sores on horses. An extraction of the stems and leaf is used for gastro-intestinal complaints and to induce milk yield in cattle. A potent anabolic steroid has

been isolated from this plant which has proved most effective in bone fracture healing, inducing early regeneration and quicker mineralisation (Hutchings et. al, 1996).

Cissus quadrangularis

The **Pink Ink Flower** (**Cycnium tubulosum ssp. montanum**) is one of the most common and noticeable ground covers or low-growing herbs on the Short Grass Plains. Leaves are linear-lanceolate, often toothed. The flowers are large (4cm to 5cm) and bright pink with yellow centres. They are called Ink Flowers because they turn bluish with age, not because they produce ink. The

plant grows mainly in black cotton soils and is a semi-parasite, parasitising on grass roots. An extraction of this plant is often used as an emetic love charm.

Pink Ink Flower

The **White Ink Flower** (**Cycnium tubulosum ssp. tubulosum**) is the white version of the previous species. The flowers are slightly smaller (3cm to 4cm) but they also have yellow centres. The pink and white plants often grow together.

White Ink Flower

The **Fireball Lily** or **Royal Shaving Brush** (**Scadoxus multiflorus**) belongs to the lily family and has bright red flowers borne on a single stem on round flowerheads. It is very attractive and appears just before the first rains in rocky areas, riverine forest, grassland, often in the shade of trees and at the edges of termite heaps. It grows from a bulb that is quite deep beneath the surface. It occurs from sea level to 2 700m. It is not very common but can be seen in virtually any vegetation type. The plant is poisonous but is used in moderate measures as a medicine. The bulb juice is used to treat external wounds and scabies.

VEGETATION

It is also taken orally for colds and asthma. The slimy juice is applied to the groin and vagina of a cow to induce birth. The juice is also applied to the udder of a cow to improve milk yield. The macerated bulb is used as fish poison and, mixed with other plants, as arrow poison.

Fireball Lily

The **Devil's Thorn** (*Tribulus terrestris*) is a much branched, prostrate herb with compound leaves and attractive yellow, five-petalled flowers. It is associated with disturbed soils and is most common along roadsides. It produces spiny, woody burrs which attach to shoes or hooves - a very effective way of dispersal. Some tribes use these thorns as an initiation test by covering an area with the thorns and getting the young men to walk over it barefoot without showing any outward sign of pain.

Devils Thorn

GRASSES

INTERESTING FACTS AND USES

Amongst the grasses, the most commonly represented genera on the Short Grass Plains are the **Love Grasses** (*Eragrostis spp.*), the **Finger Grasses** (*Digitaria macroblephara*), the **Drop Seed Grasses** (*Sporobolus iocladus*) and **Mat Grass** (*Andropogon greenwayi*). All these grasses are very high in nutrition and they are adapted to germinate soon after the first rains. Because of the high mineral content of the volcanic soils of the Short

Andropogon greenwayi

Grass Plains and the solidified layers in the soil that hold the water near the surface, the plains have a high grass yield and can support large populations of herbivores during the rainy season. One of the more common grasses in disturbed places along roads, is *Pennisetum mezianum*. The grass can be recognised by the leaf clusters along the stem.

Digitaria macroblephara

Pennisetum mezianum

Grasses on the Short Grass Plains of the NCA

V E G E T A T I O N

Tree check list

VEGETATION

The Red Thorn (Acacia lahai)

Fever Tree (Acacia xanthophloea)

Black Thorn (Acacia mellifera)

Black Thorn (Acacia mellifera)

Umbrella Thorn (Acacia tortilis)

Umbrella Thorn (Acacia tortilis)

Peacock Flower Tree (Albizia gummifera)

Peacock Flower Tree (Albizia gummifera)

Tree check list continued

Cape Chestnut (Calodendrum capense)

Cape Chestnut (Calodendrum capense)

Pillarwood (Cassipourea malosana)

Pillarwood (Cassipourea malosana) with Lichens (Usnea sp.)

Wild Caper Bush (Capparis tomentosa)

Wild Caper Bush (Capparis tomentosa)

Commiphora (Commiphora trothae)

Commiphora (Commiphora trothae)

VEGETATION

93

Tree check list continued

VEGETATION

Broad-leaved Croton (Croton macrostachyus) ⬌ *Broad-leaved Croton (Croton macrostachyus)*

Sickle Bush (Dichrostachys cinerea) ⬌ *Sickle Bush (Dichrostachys cinerea)*

Steudner's Dracaena (Dracaena steudneri) *Banana Plant (Ensete ventricosum)*

Tree Euphorbia (Euphorbia bussei) *Candelabra Tree (Euphorbia candelabrum)*

Tree check list continued

Strangler Fig (Ficus thonningii)

Strangler Fig (Ficus thonningii)

Hygenia (Hygenia abyssinica)

Hygenia (Hygenia abyssinica)

Nuxia (Nuxia congesta)

Nuxia (Nuxia congesta)

Quinine Tree (Rauvolfia caffra)

Quinine Tree (Rauvolfia caffra)

VEGETATION

Shrub check list

Buddleiya polystachya

Crassocephalum mannii

Crassocephalum mannii

*Canary Flower
(Crotalaria agatiflora)*

*Giant St. John's Wart
(Hypericum revolutum)*

*Giant Vernonia
(Vernonia auriculifera)*

Wild flower check list – green

*Milkweed
(Asclepias fruticosa)*

*Wild Asparagus
(Asparagus sp.)*

*Giant Seage
(Cyperus immensus)*

*Mother-in-law's Tongue
(Sanseveria ehrenbergiana)*

*Mother-in-law's Tongue
(Sanseveria sp.)*

*Old Mans Beard
(Usnea sp.)*

Small Mountian Fern

Mountain Fern

VEGETATION

Wild flower check list – white

Cyathula polycephala

White Ink Flower
(Cycnium tubulosum)

Cyperus obtusiflorus

Larkspur
(Delphinium leroyi)

Pretty Lady
(Gynandropsis gynandra)

Scorpion Flower
(Heliotropium steudneri)

Hibiscus flavifolius

Hibiscus fuscus

Bushman's tea
(Lippia javanica)

Long-tube Morning Glory
(Ipomoea longituba)

Smelly Cucumber
(Momordica foetida)

Ornithogalum cameronii

Pavetta sp.

Tattoo Plant
(Plumbago zeylanica)

Ruellia
(Ruellia patula)

Sambucus africana

VEGETATION

97

Wild flower check list - yellow

Toilet Paper Bush / Elephant's Ear
(Abutilon angulatum)

Abutilon rehmannii

Aeschynomene schimperi

Leopard Orchard
(Ansellia africana)

Aspilia mossambicensis

Clematis sp.

Edible-stemmed Vine
(Cissus quadrangularis)

Conyza newii

Crassocephalum montuosum

Hirpicium
(Hirpicium diffusum)

Lotus Lily
(Nymphaea lotus)

Pavonia
(Pavonia senegaleisis)

Golden Shower Climber
(Senecio hadiense)

Khaki Weed
(Tagetes minuta)

Devil's Thorn
(Tribulus terrestris)

Verbascum
brevipedicellatum

Wild flower check list – orange and red

Aloe
(Aloe secundiflora)

Aloe
(Aloe volkensii)

Buddleiya polystachya

Desmodium repandum

Emilia coccinea

Gladiolus
(Gladiolus natalensis)

Flame Lily
(Gloriosa superba)

Gynura scandens
(formerly Senecio sereti)

Everlasting Flowers
(Helichryssum sp.)

Hibiscus aponeurus

Kalanchoe lanceolata

Kleinia abyssinica

Red Hot Poker
(Kniphofia thomsonii)

Woolly Lion's Paw
(Leonotis mollissima)

Lion's Paw
(Leonotis nepetifolia)

Fireball Lily, Royal Shaving Brush (Scadoxus multiflorus)

VEGETATION

Wild flower check list – pink and purple

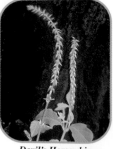

Devil's Horsewhip
(Achyranthus aspera)

Barleria argentea

Bothriocline tomentosum

Carduus sp.

Commelina benguallensis

Commicarpus pedunculosus

Pink Ink Flower
(Cycnium tubulosum)

Cynoglossum coeruleum

Cystemon hispidum

Erigeron karvinskianus

Floscopa glomerata

Purple Lady
(Gutenbergia cordifolia)

Jute Fibre Hibiscus
(Hibiscus cannabinus)

Impatiens hochstetteri

Impatiens meruensis

Indigophora
(Indigophora sp.)

VEGETATION

Jaeger's Morning Glory
(*Ipomoea jaegeri*)

Ipomoea wightii

Lantana
(*Lantana camara*)

Purple Lantana
(*Lantana trifolia*)

Nepeta azurea

Blue Water Lily
(*Nymphaea caerulea*)

Wild Basil
(*Ocimumn sp.*)

Pavonia urens

Pentas zanzebarica

Wild Sesame
(*Sesamum angustifolium*)

Sodom Apple
(*Solanum incanum*)

*Trifolium burchellianum
ssp. johnstonii*

Trifolium rueppellianum

Verbena bonariensis

Giant Vernonia
(*Vernonia auriculifera*)

Cornflower-blue Vernonia
(*Vernonia glabra*)

VEGETATION

101

Grasses check list

(Andropogon greenwayi)

(Digitaria macroblephara)

(Pennisetum mezianum)

Pinhole Grass
(Bothriachloa insculpta)

Pinhole Grass
(Bothriachloa insculpta)

Blue Buffalo Grass
(Cenchrus ciliaris)

Blue Buffalo Grass
(Cenchrus ciliaris)

Rhodes Grass
(Chloris gayana)

Rhodes Grass
(Chloris gayana)

Feather-top Chloris
(Chloris virgata)

Feather-top Chloris
(Chloris virgata)

Turpentine Grass
(Cymbopogon excavatus)

Turpentine Grass
(Cymbopogon excavatus)

Couch Grass
(Cynodon dactylon)

Couch Grass
(Cynodon dactylon)

Crow's Foot Grass
(Dactyloctenium aegyptium

Crow's Foot Grass
(Dactyloctenium aegyptium

Grasses check list continued

Goose Grass
(Eleusine coracana) — *Goose Grass*
(Eleusine coracana) — *Highland Tussock Grass*
(Eleusine jaegeri) — *Highland Tussock Grass*
(Eleusine jaegeri)

Spear Grass
(Heteropogon contortus) — *Spear Grass*
(Heteropogon contortus) — *Red Thatching Grass*
(Hyparrhenia rufa) — *Red Thatching Grass*
(Hyparrhenia rufa)

Velvet Grass
(Melenis repens) — *Velvet Grass*
(Melenis repens) — *Salt Grass*
(Odyssea sp.) — *Salt Grass*
(Odyssea sp.)

Buffalo Grass
(Panicum maximum) — *Buffalo Grass*
(Panicum maximum) — *(Pennisetum*
sphacelatum) — *(Pennisetum*
sphacelatum)

VEGETATION

VEGETATION

Cat's Tail Grass
(Perotis patens)

Cat's Tail Grass
(Perotis patens)

Common Reed
(Phragmites mauritianus)

Common Reed
(Phragmites mauritianus)

Herring-bone Grass
(Pogonarthria squarrosa)

Herring-bone Grass
(Pogonarthria squarrosa)

Bur-bristle Grass
(Setaria verticillata)

Bur-bristle Grass
(Setaria verticillata)

Wild Sorghum Grass
(Sorghum versicolor)

Wild Sorghum Grass
(Sorghum versicolor)

Pan Dropseed
(Sporobolus iocladus)

Pan Dropseed
(Sporobolus iocladus)

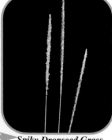

Spiky Dropseed Grass
(Sporobolus spicatus)

Spiky Dropseed Grass
(Sporobolus spicatus)

Red Oat Grass
(Themeda triandra)

Red Oat Grass
(Themeda triandra)

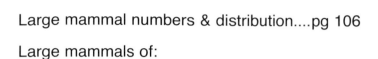

Leopard

ANIMALS – MAMMALS

NUMBER OF SPECIES IN THE NCA

Some 115 species of mammals have been recorded in the Ngorongoro Conservation Area, 55 of which occur in the Ngorongoro Crater as well (Swynnerton, et. al, 1993). The two main areas for game viewing, apart from the Ngorongoro Crater, are on the Short Grass Plains west of the Gol Mountains and at Lake Ndutu. In the sections below, estimated animal numbers are supplied for the different large mammal species. The numbers are based on a census done in 1992. Take note that there are seasonal and annual variations.

THE SHORT GRASS PLAINS

The Short Grass Plains become the breeding and feeding ground for about two million animals during the rainy season. They can be seen from about December to April. The most numerous animals on the plains are by far the Wildebeest, their population varying between one million and 1,6 million. Zebras are the second most common plains animal and their number for the Serengeti Ecosystem is estimated at ±260 000. Eland, Grant's Gazelle and Thomson's Gazelle are all common on the plains during the rainy season. After the rains the bulk of the migratory herds move on to the tall grass areas in the north, where there is permanent water. At this time, the plains become almost completely devoid of game, except for a number of Grant's Gazelles, which are not water dependent, and a few Thomson's Gazelles. Some predators remain on the Short Grass Plains after the migration has moved on, especially females with young. Others, especially young adults, follow the migration.

Eland and Thomson's Gazelle on the Short Grass Plains

LAKE NDUTU

Lake Ndutu becomes alive with Wildebeests and Zebras during the rainy season. Giraffes are always plentiful as they favour the *Acacia* plant communities which are abundant in the area. There are resident populations of Lions, Cheetahs and Hyenas at Lake Ndutu.

Wildebeest migration

THE NGORONGORO CRATER

Animal movements into and within the Ngorongoro Crater There is a resident population of animals in the Ngorongoro Crater that varies in number from 20 000 to 25 000. The population seems to remain fairly stable, with seasonal variations. The Wildebeests and Zebras are the most numerous and their numbers increase during the dry season - the reverse of what happens on the plains. On the other hand, Elephant, Eland and Waterbuck populations tend to increase during the rainy season. Animals move freely in and out of the crater, making use of animal footpaths and cattle tracks, mainly on the western and less steep side. During the rainy season the grazers are spread throughout the crater but during the dry season they concentrate in areas where the grass is green, such as on slope edges and around the Mandusi and Gorigor Swamps.

Animals that do not occur in the Ngorongoro Crater All the large mammals that occur in the rest of the NCA occur inside the crater with the exception of **Giraffe**, **Impala** and **Topi** which are all adapted to arid areas and do not favour the highlands. The Giraffe is quite capable of negotiating the cattle tracks in and out of the crater but their absence is mostly due to the lack of their favourite food species - notably the Umbrella Thorn (*Acacia tortilis*) and the Sweet Thorn (*Acacia nilotica*).

The mega-herbivores Elephant bulls are common, especially in the Lerai Forest area and in the Mandusi and Gorigor Swamps. The breeding herds occur in the highland forests and do not come into the crater. There are about 20 to 45 elephant bulls in the crater, depending on the season. They have exceptionally large tusks because of the high phosphorous quality of the soils and plants (see pg 33 for details).

Elephant bull in Crater

Hippos occur in the permanent fresh water pools and in the swamps. Hippos are exclusively grazers and their numbers depend on the availability of grass. They occur in the fresh water swamps in the crater - Mandusi and Gorigor Swamps - and in the Ngoitokitok Dam. Hippos come out to graze at night and on cool days. Their population is estimated at about 120 in the crater.

Hippo and baby

Rhinos were once common in the NCA but today they are very rare. In 1966 there were 108 Rhinos in the Ngorongoro Crater - about one Rhino per 3,1km^2. In the Olduvai Gorge 69 Rhinos were counted at this time. After 1975 Rhino poaching increased dramatically in northern Tanzania as a direct result of the growing international demand for Rhino horn. Rhino horn was, and still is, used in the Far East to prepare aphrodisiacs and in Yemen to make dagger handles - a kind of status symbol. By 1980 the Ngorongoro Rhinos declined from 30 to 25 animals. Not a single Rhino survived in the Olduvai Gorge area. In 1993 there was a further decline and only 14 to 18 Rhinos were counted in the Ngorongoro Crater. It was time for drastic steps. In November 1993 the Ngorongoro Conservation Area Authority (NCAA) and the Frankfurt Zoological Society (FZS) jointly devised a project proposal for the conservation of Rhinos in the Ngorongoro Crater - the Black Rhino Protection Programme. Today, they are guarded 24 hours per day and each is fitted with a tracking device that enables rangers to know their locality at any time. In May 2000 the Rhino population of the Ngorongoro Crater had increased to 17 animals even though three were lost to natural causes and one female to poaching. Today (2006), there are ±20 Black Rhinos in the crater.

Black Rhino

ANIMALS - MAMMALS

107

Buffalo Bull

Buffalo Breeding herds of Buffalo as well as bachelor herds occur inside the crater but they are also common in the highlands. It was found that Buffalo numbers inside the crater have improved between 1986 and 1991 and the trend seems to continue. It was suggested that the higher Buffalo numbers could be linked to the exclusion of fire inside the crater after 1974. Before 1974, the crater floor was regularly burnt by the Maasai for pasture improvement and tick control. Large populations of Zebra and Wildebeest tend to keep the grass short - a situation that is unsuitable for Buffalo as they feed on the leaves of tall grasses. Once burning was no longer allowed, the grasses were able to grow to their full length - a more suitable situation for Buffaloes. A 1992 census estimated Buffalo numbers in the crater to be between 1 500 and 5 500 animals, depending on the season. Wet season populations are much higher than dry season populations.

Zebras Zebras are extremely successful as a herbivore species. The presence of top and bottom incisors enable them to feed on tall and short grasses giving them the ability to nip off tough grass stems. They form one-stallion harems in very tightly formed units. The stallion is aggressive in defending his harem from other males and predators. During the migration, the harems unite and move in huge herds to more suitable grazing grounds. As soon as food becomes scarce, they split up again. A large portion of the Zebras seen during the rainy season in the Ngorongoro Crater, are resident.

Zebra

One can tell their resident status by the fact that they are totally relaxed around vehicles, something that they see daily. In fact, they will often not even give way to a vehicle. During the dry season their numbers escalate as a certain portion of the migratory herd move into the crater instead of moving north.

The Large cats The **Lion** population inside the crater is estimated at between 50 and 100 individuals. As they are territorial and resident, inbreeding could pose a problem but there is at least some movement in and out of the crater, especially amongst younger males. Lions form prides with one or two males, usually brothers, and between five to ten females. Males reign for one to three years (mostly from age five to age eight) after which they are ousted by younger, stronger Lions.

Lions in the crater

Cheetahs are not commonly seen but they have been recorded. The Cheetah is the fastest land animal, being able to run up to 120kph over a distance of 100m. They need open spaces to hunt. Cheetahs are mainly diurnal and they prey mostly on Thomson's Gazelles.

Cheetah in the crater

There is probably a healthy **Leopard** population in the crater but their nocturnal and secretive behaviour makes them difficult to see. Leopards prefer heavily wooded areas as they spend much of their time in trees, from where they often hunt. They take their prey up the tree to protect it from Lions and Hyenas.

Leopards spend much of their time in trees

ANIMALS - MAMMALS

Antelope The most common antelope in the crater is the **Wildebeest.** Some Wildebeest do breed inside the crater and stay there all year round, but the majority breed on the plains. When the bulk of the migration move northwards, some opt to enter the crater to see the dry season through. There are thus more Wildebeests to be seen during the dry season inside the crater. Their numbers are estimated at between 7 000 and 10 000.

Wildebeest

Grant's Gazelle, Thomson's Gazelle and **Coke's Hartebeest (Kongoni)** are all common in the crater. There are between 800 and 1 300 Grant's Gazelle, about 1 200 Thomson's Gazelle and about 160 Kongoni on the crater floor, with seasonal variations. **Eland** are not common, usually numbering less than 20. The **Defassa Waterbuck** can be seen in the Gorigor and Mandusi Swamps.

The dog family The **Hyena** population is estimated at ±400 and they form territorial clans of about 50 animals each. Hyenas live in underground burrows and come out at night to scavenge and hunt. They have the strongest jaws of all predators, enabling them to crush bones. The high calcium content of the bones result in droppings that turn bright white on drying. The very rare striped Hyena also occurs in the crater.

The three **Jackal** species that occur in the crater are the Side-striped, the Black-backed and the Golden Jackal, the latter being the most numerous. Jackals mainly scavenge but they also hunt down small mammals and baby antelope. They are all nocturnal but after a rain storm, one can often see them frolicking about.

At present there are no **African Hunting Dogs** in the crater but during the mid-sixties they were common. See box opposite for details.

AFRICAN HUNTING DOG

The **African Hunting Dog** occurs on the 1994 IUCN (International Union for Conservation of Nature and Natural Resources) Red List of threatened animals as well as on the CITES (Convention on International Trade in Endangered Species) list of animals threatened with extinction. It is almost unthinkable that Hunting Dogs were shot on site, as vermin, in wildlife parks all over Africa from the early 1900s to as late as the 1960s. In the late 1960s some 153 Hunting Dogs roamed the Serengeti Plains. In 1970, 12 packs with 95 adults were counted and in 1978 a dramatic drop was recorded - only seven packs with 26 adults. In the early 1980s only one pack remained on the plains (Estes, 1991). Today, hunting dogs are not seen at all on the plains.

Why the sharp decline? Firstly, their successful survival depends on large packs. Hunting Dog packs have only one alpha male and one alpha female that breed. The rest of the pack are helpers. Unlike most sociable mammals, Hunting Dog males remain in the natal pack and the females emigrate. All members partake in the raising of the pups and after a hunt they will all regurgitate food to the young ones. Secondly, the unusually large populations of Lions and Hyenas on the Short Grass Plains, posed a great threat to the Hunting Dog as both species kill them without provocation. Thirdly, Hunting Dogs are extremely vulnerable to various canine diseases carried by domestic dogs, such as distemper.

African Hunting Dog

ANIMALS - MAMMALS

Mammal check list

Take note: *Where there is a significant difference in the male and female animal, a photograph of the head of the opposite sex will be provided (where available). Otherwise, differences will be pointed out.*

Abbreviations: Sw: Swahili; **Ger:** German; **Fr:** French. **Height:** Shoulder height. **Length:** From nose to rump excluding tail. **Sex diff:** Sexual difference. **Soc. Org:** Social organisation.

Mega-herbivores

E: African Elephant   Sw: Tembo

African Elephant *(Loxodonto africana)*
Sw: Tembo **Ger:** Grosselephant **Fr:** L' Elephant d' Afrique

Height: M 350cm; F 300cm	**Sex diff:** Males larger with rounded head and larger tusks
Weight: M 5 750kg; F 3 800kg	
Gestation: 22 months	**Habitat:** Savannah, scrub
Litter: One	**Food:** Leaves, bark, fruit, grass
Life span: 65 years	**Soc. Org:** Gregarious, herds of
Active: Day and night	10-50. Matriarchal, non-territorial

E: Black Rhinoceros   Sw: Faru

Black Rhinoceros *(Diceros bicornis)*
Sw: Faru **Ger:** Spitzmaulnashorn **Fr:** Le `Rhinocéros noir

Height: 135 - 230cm	**Sex diff:** Cows slightly larger
Weight: 700 - 1 600kg	**Habitat:** Woodland
Gestation: 15 months	**Food:** Trees, shrubs, leaves and
Litter: One	forbs (small herbs)
Life span: 40 years	**Soc. Org:** Solitary or cow & calf/
Active: Day and night	calves, territorial

E: Hippopotamus   Sw: Kiboko

Hippopotamus *(Hippopotamus amphibius)*
Sw: Kiboko **Ger:** Grossflusspferd **Fr:** L'Hippopotame amphibié

Height: M 150 cm; F 144 cm	**Sex diff:** Males larger
Weight: M ± 2 300kg, F ± 1 900	**Habitat:** Aquatic, grassland
Gestation: 8 months	**Food:** Grass
Litter: One	**Soc. Org:** Gregarious with one
Life span: ± 40 years	dominent male, territorial
Active: Day and night	

Buffalo, Zebra and Giraffe

E: Buffalo Sw: Mbogo

Buffalo *(Syncerus caffer)*
Sw: Mbogo/Nyati **Ger:** Kaffernbüffel **Fr:** Le Buffle d `Afrique

Height: 140 - 170cm	**Sex diff:** Horns of male have thicker boss
Weight: M 785kg; F 715kg	
Gestation: 11 months	**Habitat:** Woodland, tall grass areas
Litter: One	**Food:** Tall grasses, leaves & shoots
Life span: ± 23 years	**Soc. Org:** Gregarious, territorial
Active: Day and night	in large home ranges

Zebra *(Equus quagga boehmi)*
Sw: Punda milia **Ger:** Steppenzebra **Fr:** Le Zébre de steppe

Height: ± 134cm

Weight: M ± 290kg; F ± 210kg

Gestation: 12 months

Litter: One

Life span: 35 years

Active: Day and night

Sex diff: Males more stout

Habitat: Grass and savannah woodland

Food: Tall and short grasses

Soc. Org: Harems with one male and ± 3-6 females, non-territorial

E: Zebra   Sw: Punda milia

Giraffe *(Giraffa camelopardalis)*
Sw: Twiga **Ger:** Giraffe **Fr:** La Giraffe

Height: ± 3m to the shoulder; 4.5 - 5m total

Weight: M ± 1 850kg; F ± 825kg

Gestation: 15 months

Litter: One

Life span: 28 years

Active: Day and night

Food: *Acacia* leaves, pods

Sex diff: Males more heavily built, horns thicker

Habitat: *Acacia* savannah woodland

Soc. Org: Loose herd structure, groups of ± 4 - 20, non-territorial

E: Giraffe   Sw: Twiga

The Cat family

Lion *(Panthera leo)*
Sw: Simba **Ger:** Löwe **Fr:** Le Lion

Height: M 115cm; F 91cm

Weight: M ± 220kg; F ± 150kg

Gestation: 3,5 months

Litter: 1 - 4

Life span: 20 years

Active: Mostly nocturnal

Sex. diff: Males larger with mane

Habitat: Varied - forest to desert

Food: Meat, mainly ungulates

Soc. Org: Prides of 2 - 30 animals with one dominant male or two brothers, territorial

E: Lion (male)   Sw: Simba

Leopard *(Panthera pardus)*
Sw: Chui **Ger:** Leopard **Fr:** La Panthère d'Afrique

Height: 65cm

Weight: M ± 60kg; F ± 40kg

Gestation: 3 months

Litter: 2 - 3

Life span: 20 years

Active: Nocturnal

Sex diff: Males larger

Habitat: Woodland, riverine forest, mountains, kopjes

Food: Meat, middle-sized ungulates and small mammals

Soc. Org: Solitary, territorial

E: Leopard   Sw: Chui

ANIMALS – MAMMALS

The Cat family continued

E: Cheetah   Sw: Msongo/Duma

Cheetah *(Acinonyx jubatus)*
Sw: Msongo/Duma **Ger:** Gepard **Fr:** Le Guépard

Height: 86cm	**Sex diff:** Males slightly heavier
Weight: M ± 50kg; F ± 42kg	**Habitat:** Open woodland & grassland plains
Gestation: 3 months	
Litter: 1 - 5	**Food:** Meat, smaller ungulates and other small animals and birds
Life span: 16 years	
Active: Diurnal	**Soc. Org:** Pairs, mothers with cubs, solitary, non-territorial

E: Serval   Sw: Mondo

Serval *(Felis serval)*
Sw: Mondo **Ger:** Servalkatze **Fr:** Le Serval

Height: 56cm	**Sex diff:** Males slightly heavier
Weight: M 14kg; F 9kg	**Habitat:** Moist bushland, riverine forest
Gestation: 2 months	
Litter: 1 - 4	**Food:** Small mammals and birds
Life span: 13-20 years	**Soc. Org:** Solitary or mother with young
Active: Mainly nonctural	

E: Caracal   Sw: Simba mangu

Caracal *(Felis caracal)*
Sw: Simba mangu **Ger:** Wüstenluchs **Fr:** Le Caracal

Height: 43cm	**Sex diff:** Males slightly heavier
Weight: M ± 15kg; F ± 10kg	**Habitat:** Dry *Acacia* bushland, semi-desert and rocky areas
Gestation: 2 months	
Litter: 2 - 4	**Food:** Small mammals and birds
Life span: 11 years	**Soc. Org:** Solitary or mother with young
Active: Mainly nocturnal	

E: African Wild Cat   Sw: Paka mwitu

African Wild Cat *(Felis silvestris lybica)*
Sw: Paka mwitu **Ger:** Wildkatze **Fr:** Le Chat gante' d 'Afrique

Height: 25cm	**Sex diff:** Males slightly larger
Weight: M 5kg; F 4kg	**Habitat:** Varied, requires tall grass or rocks
Gestation: 2 months	
Litter: 1 - 5	**Food:** Small rodents, birds, insects
Life span: Not known	**Soc. Org:** Solitary or mother with young
Active: Mainly nocturnal	

ANIMALS – MAMMALS

Mammal check list

The Pig family

Warthog *(Phacochoerus aethiopicus)*
Sw: Ngiri **Ger:** Warzenschwein **Fr:** Le Phacochére

Height: M 70cm; F 60cm
Weight: M ± 100kg; F ± 60kg
Gestation: 5,5 months
Litter: 1 - 8
Life span: 20 years
Active: Diurnal

Sex diff: Males larger with 2 pairs of warts, female 1 pair
Habitat: Open woodland & water
Food: Roots, rhizomes, fruit, grass
Soc. Org: Family groups of 4 - 10, matriarchal, non-territorial

E: Warthog   Sw: Ngiri

Bushpig *(Potamochoerus larvatus)*
Sw: Nguruwe **Ger:** Buschschwein **Fr:** Le Potamochére d` Afrique

Height: 70 - 100cm
Weight: M 120kg; F 70kg
Gestation: 4 months
Litter: 2 - 3
Life span: 20 years
Active: Nocturnal

Sex diff: Males larger
Habitat: Woodland, riverine forest, mountains
Food: Roots, rhizomes, fruit, grass and they scavenge
Soc. Org: Solitary

E: Bushpig   Sw: Nguruwe

The Dog family

Spotted Hyena *(Crocuta crocuta)*
Sw: Fisi madoa **Ger:** Fleckenhyäne **Fr:** Le Hyèna tachetée

Height: 77cm
Weight: M 63kg; F 70kg
Gestation: 4 months
Litter: 1 - 4
Life span: 25 years
Active: Nocturnal

Sex diff: Females larger than males
Habitat: Varied, grassland or woodland and semi-desert
Food: Carrion and also hunt
Soc. Org: Gregarious, dominant female, matriarchal, territorial

E: Spotted Hyena   Sw: Fisi madoa

African Hunting Dog *(Lycaon pictus)*
Sw: Mbwa mwitu **Ger:** Hyänenhund **Fr:** Le Cynhyène

Height: 68cm
Weight: 20 - 36kg
Gestation: 2,5 months
Litter: ± 14
Life span: 12 years
Active: Diurnal

Sex diff: None
Habitat: Open woodland
Food: Meat, mammals
Soc. Org: Gregarious, packs of 6-30, dominant male and female, non-territorial

E: African Hunting Dog   Sw: Mbwa mwitu

ANIMALS - MAMMALS

113

ANIMALS – MAMMALS

E: Aardwolf   Sw: Fisi ya nkole

Burger Cillié

Aardwolf *(Protelus cristatus)*
Sw: Fisi ya nkole **Ger:** Erdwolf **Fr:** Le Protèle

Height: 50cm

Weight: 11kg

Gestation: 2,5 months

Litter: 2 - 4

Life span: 13 years

Active: Nocturnal

Sex diff: None

Habitat: Open woodland, grassland, semi-desert

Food: Harvester termites

Soc. Org: Usually solitary or mother and young, territorial

E: Golden Jackal Sw: Mbweha mgongo dhahabu

Golden Jackal *(Canis aureus)*
Sw: Mbweha mgongo dhahabu **Ger:** Goldschakal **Fr:** Le Chacal commun

Height: 43cm

Weight: 12,5kg

Gestation: 2 months

Litter: 3 - 8

Life span: 10 - 12 years

Active: Day and Night

Sex diff: None

Habitat: Open country with good cover and water

Food: Carrion, small mammals and birds, also sugarcane, maize and green crops - omnivorous

Soc. Org: Pairs for life, territorial, may form group territories

E: Side-striped Jackal Sw: Mbweha miraba

Side-striped Jackal *(Canis adustus)*
Sw: Mbweha miraba **Ger:** Streifenschakal **Fr:** Chacal à flancs rayés

Height: 39cm

Weight: M 9,7kg; F 8,7kg

Gestation: 2 - 2,5 months

Litter: 2 - 6

Life span: 11 years

Active: Day and Night

Sex diff: Males slightly larger

Habitat: Thick woodland with plenty water

Food: Carrion, fruit, hares, rodents

Soc. Org: Solitary or pairs for life, also family groups, territorial

E: Black-backed Jackal Sw: Mbweha mgongo mweusi

Black-backed Jackal *(Canis mesomelas)*
Sw: Mbweha mgongo mweusi **Ger:** Schabrackenschakal **Fr:** Le Chacal à chabraque

Height: 38cm

Weight: M 10kg; F 8kg

Gestation: 2 months

Litter: 1 - 6

Life span: 13 years

Active: Day and Night

Sex diff: Males slightly larger

Habitat: Very well adapted in all habitats

Food: Carrion, small mammals

Soc. Org: Solitary or pairs for life, also family groups, territorial

The Dog family continued

Bat-eared Fox *(Otocyon megalotis)*
Sw: Mbweha masikio **Ger:** Löffelhund **Fr:** L'Otocyon

Height: 25 -30cm
Weight: M 3,8kg; F 4,2kg
Gestation: 2 months
Litter: 2 - 6
Life span: 12 years
Active: Day and Night
Sex diff: Females slightly larger

Habitat: Open dry bush or semi-desert
Food: Mostly termites, insects, occasionally small rodents
Soc. Org: Pairs or family of up to 8, territorial

E: Bat-eared Fox Sw: Mbweha masikio

The large Antelopes

Eland *(Taurotragus oryx)*
Sw: Pofu **Ger:** Elanantilope **Fr:** L'Eland/'Elan du Cap

Height: M 170cm; F 145cm
Weight: M ± 800kg; ± F 480kg
Gestation: 9 months
Litter: One
Life span: 25 years
Active: Mainly diurnal
Sex diff: Males much larger

Habitat: Varied, from open plains to mountains to semi-deserts
Food: Mainly leaves, fruit, also grass in summer
Soc. Org: Gregarious, small herds of 8-12 or very large herds. Very large home ranges

E: Eland Sw: Pofu

Defassa Waterbuck *(Kobus ellipsiprymnus)*
Sw: Kuro **Ger:** Wasserbuck **Fr:** Le Cobe Defassa

Height: M 135cm; F 120cm
Weight: M ± 250kg; F ± 175kg
Gestation: 8,5 months
Litter: One
Life span: ± 18 years
Active: Day and Night

Sex diff: Males larger with horns
Habitat: Riverine canopy woodland, always near water
Food: Medium grasses
Soc. Org: Harem herds of ± 6 females and one dominant male, territorial, satellite males

E: Defassa Waterbuck Sw: Kuro

Coke's Hartebeest *(Alcelaphus buselaphus cokei)*
Sw: Kongoni **Ger:** Kuhantilope **Fr:** Le Bubale

Height: 132cm
Weight: M 170kg; F 150kg
Gestation: 8 months
Litter: One
Life span: 19 years
Active: Mainly diurnal

Sex diff: Males slightly larger
Habitat: Bounderies of grassy plains and woodland
Food: Grass, non-selective
Soc. Org: Harem troops

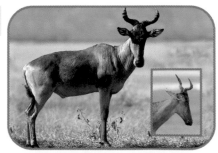
E: Coke's Hartebeest Sw: Kongoni

ANIMALS – MAMMALS

White-bearded Gnu *(Connochaetes taurinus)*
Sw: Nyumbu ya montu **Ger:** Weissbart **Fr:** Le Gnou Bleu

Height: M 150cm; F 135cm
Weight: M 250kg; F 200kg
Gestation: 8,5 months
Litter: One
Life span: 20 years
Active: Mainly diurnal

Sex diff: Males larger
Habitat: Short grass plains, open woodland
Food: Grass, preferably short grass
Soc. Org: Gregarious, one bull and several females, territorial during rut

E: White-bearded Gnu Sw: Nyumbu ya montu

The middle-sized Antelopes

Grant's Gazelle *(Gazella granti)*
Sw: Swala Granti **Ger:** Grantgazelle **Fr:** La Gazelle de Grant

Height: M 90cm; F 83cm
Weight: M 70kg; F 50kg
Gestation: 6,5 months
Litter: One
Life span: 12 years
Active: Mainly diurnal
Sex diff: Males larger, thicker horns

Habitat: Arid areas, open grass plains with bush
Food: Grass and leaves, not water dependent
Soc. Org: Dominant male with 10 - 30 females, bachelor herds, territorial

E: Grant's Gazelle Sw: Swala Granti

Thomson's Gazelle *(Gazella rufifrons thomsoni)*
Sw: Swala Tomi **Ger:** Thomsongazella **Fr:** La Gazella de Thomson

Height: M 62cm; F 55cm
Weight: M 28kg; F 20kg
Gestation: 6 months
Litter: One
Life span: 10 years
Active: Mainly diurnal

Sex diff: Males larger, thicker and longer horns
Habitat: Open, short grass plains
Food: Short grass and about 10% foliage, water dependent
Soc. Org: Loose, one male, up to 60 females, bachelor herds

E: Thomson's Gazelle Sw: Swala Tomi

Impala *(Aepyceros melampus)*
Sw: Swala Pala **Ger:** Schwartzfersenantilope **Fr:** Le Pallah

Height: M 90cm; F 86cm
Weight: M 65kg; F 50kg
Gestation: 6,5 months
Litter: One
Life span: 12 years
Active: Mainly diurnal

Sex diff: Males have horns, larger than females
Habitat: Open woodland, water
Food: Grass and leaves
Soc. Org: Gregarious, dominant male, territorial during rut

E: Impala Sw: Swala Pala

The middle-sized Antelopes continued

Bushbuck *(Tragelaphus scriptus)*
Sw: Pongo **Ger:** Schirrantilope **Fr:** L'Antilope harnaché, Le Guib

Height: M 90cm; F 75cm
Weight: M 60kg; F 44kg
Gestation: 6 months
Litter: One
Life span: 11 years
Active: Day and night
Sex diff: Males have horns

Habitat: Riverine woodland, dense bush
Food: Leaves, fruit
Soc. Org: Pairs or family groups, mostly solitary, non-territorial

E: Bushbuck   Sw: Pongo

Oribi *(Ourebia ourebi)*
Sw: Taya **Ger:** Bleichböckchen **Fr:** L'Ourébie

Height: ± 58cm
Weight: M 15kg; F 17kg
Gestation: 7 months
Litter: One
Life span: 13 years
Active: Mainly diurnal

Sex diff: Males have horns, female larger
Habitat: Open grassveld
Food: Grass maintained by fire
Soc. Org: Solitary or small groups, territorial

E: Oribi   Sw: Taya

The dwarf Antelopes

Klipspringer *(Oreotragus oreotragus)*
Sw: Ngurunguru/Mbuzi mawe **Ger:** Klippspringer **Fr:** L'Oréotrague

Height: 52cm
Weight: M 12kg; F 14kg
Gestation: 7,5 months
Litter: One
Life span: 7 years
Active: Day and night

Sex diff: Males have horns
Habitat: Rocky outcrops, mountains and kopjes
Food: Leaves, fruit, herbs, shrubs
Soc. Org: Pairs or family groups, territorial

E: Klipspringer   Sw: Ngurunguru/Mbuzi mawe

Steinbok *(Raphicerus campestris)*
Sw: Dondor/Isha **Ger:** Steinböckchen **Fr:** Le Steenbok

Height: 52cm
Weight: ± 11kg
Gestation: 6 months
Litter: One, sometimes two
Life span: 7 years
Active: Day and night

Sex diff: Males have horns
Habitat: Arid, unstable areas
Food: Grass, leaves, fruit, bulbs, not water dependent
Soc. Org: Solitary, pairs or mother and young, territorial

E: Steinbok   Sw: Dondor/Isha

ANIMALS – MAMMALS

SAN PARKS

117

ANIMALS – MAMMALS

The dwarf Antelopes continued

E: Blue Duiker   Sw: Ndimba/Chesi

Blue Duiker *(Philantomba monticola)*
Sw: Ndimba/Chesi **Ger:** Blauducker **Fr:** Le Céphalophe bleu

Height: ± 35cm
Weight: M 4,7kg; F 6kg
Gestation: ± 4 months
Litter: One
Life span: ± 10 years
Active: Day and night

Sex diff: Both have horns, smaller or sometimes absent in females
Habitat: Forests
Food: Leaves, fruit
Soc. Org: Solitary or pairs, territorial

E: Kirk's Dik-dik   Sw: Dikidiki/Suguya

Kirk's Dik-dik *(Madoqua kirkii)*
Sw: Dikidiki/Suguya **Ger:** Kirkdikdik **Fr:** Le Dik-dik de kirk

Height: 39cm
Weight: 5kg
Gestation: 5,5 - 6 months
Litter: One
Life span: 9 years
Active: Day and night

Sex diff: Males have horns
Habitat: Thick woodland
Food: Leaves, fruit, not water dependent
Soc. Org: Solitary or pairs, territorial

The Primates

E: Olive Baboon   Sw: Nyani

Olive Baboon *(Papio anubis)*
Sw: Nyani **Ger:** Anubispaviaan **Fr:** Le Babouin doguer

Height: M 65cm; F 55cm
Weight: M 28kg; F 17kg
Gestation: 6 months
Litter: One
Life span: 30 - 40 years
Active: Diurnal

Sex diff: Males larger
Habitat: Woodland savannah and mountain areas
Food: Fruit, berries, insects, sometimes meat
Soc. Org: Troops of ± 70

E: Black-faced Vervet Monkey   Sw: Tumbili /Ngedere

Black-faced Vervet Monkey *(Cercopithecus aethiops)*
Sw: Tumbili /Ngedere **Ger:** Grünmeerkatze **Fr:** Le grivet

Height: M 45cm, F 80cm
Weight: M 7kg; F 5,5kg
Gestation: 6.5 months
Litter: One
Life span: 24 years
Active: Diurnal
Sex diff: Males larger, blue & red genitals

Habitat: Savannah & bush, riverine forest
Food: Fruit, berries, flowers, bark, insects, nestlings, small mammals
Soc. Org: Organised troops of 6 - 30, one dominant male

The Primates continued

Lesser Bushbaby *(Galago senegalensis subsp. braccatus)*
Sw: Komba ya Senegal **Ger:** Senegalgalago **Fr:** Galago du Sénégal

Height: 17,5cm
Weight: 150 - 250g
Gestation: 4 months
Litter: 1 - 2
Active: Nocturnal
Life span: 10 years

Sex diff: None
Habitat: Acacia woodland
Food: Gum, grasshoppers, moths, spiders
Soc. Org: Gregarious, territorial

E: Lesser Bushbaby Sw: Komba ya Senegal

Greater Bushbaby *(Otolemur/Galago crassicaudatus)*
Sw: Komba ya Miombo **Ger:** Riesengalago **Fr:** Le Galago à queue épaisse

Height: 37 cm
Weight: M 1,22 kg; F 1,13 kg
Gestation: 4 months
Litter: 1 - 2
Active: Nocturnal
Life span: 14 years

Sex diff: Males slightly larger
Habitat: Woodland and forest, especially Miombo woodland
Food: Fruit, gum, insects, birds
Soc. Org: Partly solitary, family groups sleep together, territorial

E: Greater Bushbaby Sw: Komba Miombo

The Hydraxes

Tree Hyrax *(Dendrohyrax arboreus)*
Sw: Perere **Ger:** Waldschliefer **Fr:** L daman d'arbre

Length: 40 - 60cm
Weight: M 3,5kg; F 2,4kg
Gestation: 8 months
Litter: 1-2
Life span: 12 years
Active: Nocturnal

Sex diff: None
Habitat: Mountains, moist savannah forest
Food: Leaves, fruit, herbage, grass, insects, eggs, lizards
Soc. Org: Usually in pairs with young or solitary, territorial

E: Tree Hyrax Sw: Perere

Rock Hyrax *(Heterohyrax brucei)*
Sw: Pimbi **Ger:** Steppenschliefer **Fr:** Le daman de steppe

Length: 40 - 57cm
Weight: M 2,75kg; F 2,5kg
Gestation: 8 months
Litter: 1-2
Life span: 12 years
Active: Diurnal

Sex diff: None
Habitat: Plains to mountains, kopjes, savannah
Food: Mostly leaves, also herbage and grass
Soc. Org: Usually in pairs with young or solitary, territorial

E: Rock Hyrax Sw: Pimbi

SAN PARKS

ANIMALS – MAMMALS

ANIMALS - MAMMALS

Hares

E: Red Rock Hare   Sw: Sungura

Red Rock Hare *(Pronolagus sp.)*
Sw: Sungura **Ger:** Rothase **Fr:** Le Lièvre roux

Length: 43 - 53cm
Weight: 1,3 - 2,5kg
Gestation: 4 weeks
Litter: 1 - 2
Life span: Not known
Active: Nocturnal

Sex diff: None
Habitat: Rocky areas with bush cover like cliffs
Food: Grass and herbage
Soc. Org: Small groups or solitary, forage alone

E: Cape Hare   Sw: Sungura

Cape Hare *(Lepus capensis)*
Sw: Sungura **Ger:** Kaphase **Fr:** Le Lièvre du Cap

Length: 45 -75cm
Weight: M 1,6kg; F 1,9kg
Gestation: 5 weeks
Litter: 1 - 3
Life span: 5 years
Active: Nocturnal

Sex diff: Females slightly larger
Habitat: Open grassland with patches of tall grass
Food: Short grass, herbs
Soc. Org: Solitary, tolerates neighbours

Mongooses

E: Dwarf Mongoose   Sw: Kitafe

Dwarf Mongoose *(Helogale parvula)*
Sw: Kitafe **Ger:** Zwergichneumon **Fr:** La Mangouste nain

Length: 18 - 28cm
Weight: ± 280g
Gestation: 8 weeks
Litter: 2 - 4
Life span: ± 6 years
Active: Diurnal

Sex diff: None
Habitat: Thickets and woodland with termitaria
Food: Termites, worms, snails, insects
Soc. Org: Form colonies of 10 or more

E: Slender Mongoose   Sw: Nguchiro

Slender Mongoose *(Galerella sanguinea)*
Sw: Nguchiro **Ger:** Schlankichneumon **Fr:** La Mangouste rouge

Length: 25 - 40cm
Weight: M 400-900g; F 350-500g
Gestation: Not known
Litter: 1 - 2
Life span: ± 8 years
Active: Diurnal

Sex diff: None
Habitat: Varies from desert to rainforest, very adaptable
Food: Termites, beetles, locusts, insects, eggs, mice
Soc. Org: Solitary

Mongooses continuued

White-tailed Mongoose *(Ichneumia albicauda)*
Sw: Karambago   **Ger:** Weisschwanzichneumon
Fr: La Mangouste à queu blanche

Length: ± 60cm
Weight: M 4,5kg; F 3,5kg
Gestation: Not known
Litter: 1 - 3
Life span: 12,5 years
Active: Nocturnal

Sex diff: Male slightly heavier
Habitat: Woodlands with plenty water, along rivers
Food: Insects, mice, frogs, birds, snails, fruit
Soc. Org: Solitary or pairs

E: White-tailed Mongoose Sw: Karambago

Banded Mongoose *(Mungos mungo)*
Sw: Nguchiro   **Ger:** Zebramanguste   **Fr:** La Mangue rayée

Length: 30-45cm
Weight: 1,5 - 2,2kg
Gestation: 8 weeks
Litter: 2 - 8
Life span: ± 8 years
Active: Diurnal

Sex diff: None
Habitat: Riverine forest or dense thornveld
Food: Insects, reptiles, eggs, fruit, snails
Soc. Org: Gregarious, colonies of 30 or more

E: Banded Mongoose Sw: Nguchiro

Other small Mammals

Antbear / Aardvark *(Orycteropus afer)*
Sw: Muhanga/Kukukifuku   **Ger:** Erdferkel   **Fr:** Le Orycterope

Height: 61cm
Weight: M 70kg; F 50kg
Gestation: 7 months
Litter: One
Life span: 18 years
Active: Nocturnal

Sex diff: Males slightly larger
Habitat: Very adaptable
Food: Termites and ant
Soc. Org: Solitary

E: Antbear / Aardvark Sw: Muhanga / Kukukifuku

Pangolin *(Manis temmincki)*
Sw: Kaka/Kakakuona   **Ger:** Steppenschuppentier
Fr: Pangolin de Temminck

Length: 81cm
Weight: 4,5 - 14,5 kg
Gestation: 4,5 months
Litter: One
Life span: 12 years
Active: Nocturnal

Sex diff: None
Habitat: Sandy soil in dry bushveld
Food: Termites and ant
Soc. Org: Solitary

E: Pangolin Sw: Kakakuona

SAN PARKS

ANIMALS - MAMMALS

Other small Mammals continued

ANIMALS – MAMMALS

E: Porcupine   Sw: Nungunungu

Porcupine *(Hystrix africaeaustralis)*
Sw: Nungunungu **Ger:** Südafrika-Stachelschwein
Fr: Le Porc-épique de l'Afrique du Sud

Length: 84cm
Weight: 20 - 25kg
Gestation: 3 months
Litter: 1 - 4
Life span: 8 years
Active: Nocturnal

Sex diff: Females heavier
Habitat: Woodland and scrub
Food: Roots, bulbs, rhizomes, vegetables, fruit
Soc. Org: Loose groups of ± 4

E: Spring Hare   Sw: Kamendegere

Spring Hare *(Pedetes capensis)*
Sw: Kamendegere **Ger:** Springhase **Fr:** Le Lièrre sauteur

Length: 40cm + tail 40cm
Weight: 2,5 - 3,8kg
Gestation: 2 months
Litter: One
Life span: 7 years
Active: Nocturnal

Sex diff: None
Habitat: Near pans or higher, ground in sandy-loam soil
Food: Rhizomes, tubers, grass
Soc. Org: Solitary, or pair with young

SAN PARKS

E: Greater Canerat   Sw: Ndezi / Nkungusi

Greater Canerat *(Thryonomys swinderianus)*
Sw: Ndezi/Nkungusi **Ger:** Grosse Rohrratte **Fr:** L'Aulacode grand

Length: 50 - 60cm
Weight: 4,5 - 9kg
Gestation: 3 months
Litter: 2 - 6
Life span: 4 years
Active: Nocturnal

Sex diff: None
Habitat: Dense grass, reed beds, sedges, swamps
Food: Roots, shoots, grass stems, reeds
Soc. Org: Groups up to 12

SAN PARKS

E: Clawless Otter Sw: Fisi maji

Clawless Otter *(Aonyx capensis)*
Sw: Fisi maji **Ger:** Kapfingerotter **Fr:** La Loutre a joues blanches

Length: 80cm + tail 50cm
Weight: 15 - 22kg
Gestation: 9 months
Litter: One, rarely 2
Life span: 15 years
Active: Diurnal

Sex diff: None
Habitat: Aquatic
Food: Frogs, crabs, fish, birds, reptiles, insects
Soc. Org: Solitary or pairs, mother and baby

Honey Badger *(Mellivora capensis)*
Sw: Nyegere/Kinyegale **Ger:** Honigdachs **Fr:** Le Ratel

Height: 70cm + tail 20cm
Weight: 10 - 16kg
Gestation: 6,5 months
Litter: Usually 2
Life span: 24 years
Active: Nocturnal

Sex diff: Males are heavier
Habitat: Most habitats except true deserts
Food: Honey, fruit, birds, scorpions, reptiles
Soc. Org: Usually solitary, rarely pairs

E: Honey Badger Sw: Nyegere/Kinyegale

African Civet *(Civettictis civetta)*
Sw: Fungo/Ngawa **Ger:** Afrika-Zibetkatze **Fr:** La Civette dé Afrique

Length: 33cm + tail 25cm
Weight: 650 - 1 300g
Gestation: 5 weeks
Litter: 2-3
Life span: 5,5 years
Active: Nocturnal

Sex diff: Males larger
Habitat: Rock crevices, under piles of stones
Food: Small mammals, birds, eggs, reptiles, insects
Soc. Org: Solitary

E: Striped Polecat / Zorilla Sw: Kicheche/Kanu

African Civet *(Civettictis civetta)*
Sw: Fungo/Ngawa **Ger:** Afrika-Zibetkatze **Fr:** La Civette dé Afrique

Height: 40cm
Weight: M 11,4kg; F 14,9kg
Gestation: 2 months
Litter: 1-4
Life span: 12 years
Active: Nocturnal

Sex diff: Females larger
Habitat: Bushveld with thick undergrowth
Food: Insects, mice, fruit, reptiles and birds
Soc. Org: Solitary

E: African Civet Sw: Fungo / Ngawa

Large-spotted Genet *(Genetta tigrina)*
Sw: Kanu **Ger:** Grossfleckginsterkatze **Fr:** La genetta à grandes taches

Length: ± 45cm + tail 45cm
Weight: 1 - 3kg
Gestation: 2 months
Litter: One
Life span: 13 years
Active: Nocturnal

Sex diff: None
Habitat: Bush with plenty water
Food: Rodents, insects, birds, crabs
Soc. Org: Solitary or in pairs

E: Large-spotted Genet Sw: Kanu

SAN PARKS

ANIMALS – MAMMALS

Other small Mammals continued

Burger Cillié

E: Small-spotted Genet Sw: Kanu

Small-spotted Genet *(Genetta genetta)*
Sw: Kanu **Ger:** Gemeine Ginsterkatze **Fr:** La Genette vulgaire

Height: 15 - 20cm
Weight: M 2,5kg; F 1,7kg
Gestation: 2 months
Litter: 1-4
Life span: 15 years
Active: Nocturnal

Sex diff: None
Habitat: Open dry savannah with sufficient cover
Food: Small mammals, birds, snails, fruit, crabs
Soc. Org: Solitary

SAN PARKS

E: Hedgehog Sw: Karunguyeye

Hedgehog *(Erinaceus albiventris)*
Sw: Karunguyeye **Ger:** Weisbauchigel **Fr:** Le Hérisson à ventre blanc

Length: 17 - 23cm
Weight: 500 - 700g
Gestation: 5,5 weeks
Litter: 2 - 10, usually 5
Life span: 8 - 10 years
Active: Nocturnal

Sex diff: None
Habitat: Woodland, bushland, grassland
Food: Earthworms, insects, snails, lizards, frogs, carrion, fungi, roots
Soc. Org: Solitary, except mother with young

Rats, Mice, Gerbils & Shrews

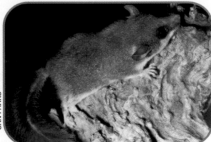

SAN PARKS

E: Dwarf Mongoose Sw: Kitafe

Woodland Dormouse *(Graphiurus murinus)*
Sw: Panya miti

Length: 80 - 110mm
Weight: 40 - 85g
Litter size: 4
Gestation: 24 days
Active: Nocturnal

Habitat: Woodland, arboreal, beehives
Food: Dead bees, honey, wax, bagworms, termites

SAN PARKS

E: Water Rat Sw: Panya

Water Rat *(Dasymys incomtus)*
Sw: Panya

Length: ± 155mm
Weight: 90 - 120g
Litter: 1 - 3
Gestation: Not known
Active: Nocturnal

Habitat: Swamps, reedbeds, Riverine vegetation
Food: Mostly vegetarian, insects

ANIMALS – MAMMALS

Pencil-tailed Tree Rat *(Thallomys paedulcus)*
Sw: Panya

Length: 140 - 150mm
Weight: 100 - 120g
Litter: Not known
Gestation: Not known
Active: At night

Habitat: Mainly Acacia trees
Food: Mainly *Acacia* seeds, pods and leaves

E: Pencil-tailed Tree Rat   Sw: Panya

Four-striped Ground Mouse *(Rhabdomys pumilio)*
Sw: Panya

Length: 100 - 120mm
Weight: 42 - 52g
Litter: 3 - 9
Gestation: ± 25 days
Active: Diurnal

Habitat: Varied, prefers grassland
Food: Omnivorous

E: Bush Rat / Red Veld Rat   Sw: Panya

Four-striped Ground Mouse *(Rhabdomys pumilio)*
Sw: Panya

Length: 100 - 120mm
Weight: 42 - 52g
Litter: 3 - 9
Gestation: ± 25 days
Active: Diurnal

Habitat: Varied, prefers grassland
Food: Omnivorous

E: Four-striped Ground Mouse   Sw: Panya

Single-striped Mouse *(Lemniscomys griselda)*
Sw: Panya

Length: 130 - 150mm
Weight: 44 - 80g
Litter: 5-7
Gestation: Not known
Active: Diurnal

Habitat: Grassland in low Acacia veld
Food: Mainly grass seeds, vegetable matter

E: Single-striped Mouse   Sw: Panya

ANIMALS - MAMMALS

SAN PARKS

125

ANIMALS – MAMMALS

Shamba Rat/Mutlimammate Mouse (Praomys natalensis)
Sw: Panya

Length: 120 - 140mm
Weight: 50 - 60g
Litter: 10 - 16, up to 24
Gestation: ± 23 days
Active: Nocturnal

Habitat: Very adaptable, mostly in woodlands
Food: Acacia seeds, pods, fruit, grass

E: Shamba Rat Sw: Panya

Pouched Mouse (Saccostomus campestris)
Sw: Panya

Length: ± 160mm
Weight: 42 - 48g
Litter: ± 3 - 5
Gestation: 20 - 21 days
Active: Nocturnal, solitary

Habitat: Varied, prefers sandy woodland
Food: Mainly seeds of shrubs and trees like *Acacia*

E: Pouched Mouse Sw: Panya

Chestnut Climbing Mouse (Dendromus mystacalis)
Sw: Panya

Length: 60 - 80mm
Weight: 7 - 14g
Litter: 3 - 5
Gestation: Not known
Active: Nocturnal

Habitat: Arboreal at low altitudes
Food: Grains and insects

E: Chestnut Climbing Mouse Sw: Panya

Grey Pygmy Climbing Mouse (Dendromus melanotis)
Sw: Panya

Length: 56 - 81mm
Weight: 4 - 12g
Litter: 3 - 5
Gestation: Not known
Active: Nocturnal

Habitat: Arboreal at low altitudes
Food: Grains and insects

E: Grey Pygmy Climbing Mouse S: Panya

Pygmy Mouse *(Mus minutoides)*
Sw: Panya

Length: 53 - 70mm

Weight: 6 - 11g

Litter: ± 4

Gestation: ± 19 days

Active: Nocturnal

Habitat: Varied from semi-desert to riverine areas

Food: Omnivorous

E: Pygmy Mouse Sw: Panya

Bushveld Gerbil *(Tatera leucogaster)*
Sw: Panya

Length: 120 - 160mm

Weight: 60 - 125g

Litter: 4 - 5

Gestation: Not known

Active: Nocturnal

Habitat: Well-drained, sandy areas, sub-Saharan areas

Food: Seeds, stems, roots, insects

E: Bushveld Gerbil   Sw: Panya

Lesser Elephant Shrew *(Elephantulus brachyrynchus)*
Sw: Sange **Ger:** Elephantenspitzmaus **Fr:** Macroscélide

Length: 210 - 280mm

Weight: 25 - 70g

Litter: 1 - 2

Gestation: ± 2 months

Active: Diurnal

Habitat: Dry scrubby bush

Food: Invertebrates

E: Lesser Elephant Shrew Sw: Sange

Lesser Red Musk Shrew *(Crocidura hirta)*
Sw: Kirukanjia

Length: 115 - 160mm

Weight: 8 - 22g

Litter: 3 - 4

Gestation: 18 days

Active: Nocturnal

Habitat: Damp areas along streams

Food: Earthworms, insects, termites

E: Lesser Red Musk Shrew Sw: Kirukanjia

ANIMALS – MAMMALS

SAN PARKS

Bats

E: Epauletted Fruit Bat   S: Popo

Epauletted Fruit Bat *(Epomophorus sp.)*
Sw: Popo

Length: 120 - 160mm
Weight: 64 - 140g
Litter: One, seldom twins
Gestation: Not known
Active: Nocturnal

Habitat: Fruit-bearing trees, riverine vegetation
Food: Wild figs, marula and all other wild fruit
Soc. Org: Gregarious

E: Common Slit-faced Bat   Sw: Popo

Common Slit-faced Bat *(Nycteris thebaica)*
Sw: Popo

Length: 92 - 120mm
Weight: 7 - 15g
Litter: One
Gestation: 5 months
Active: Nocturnal

Habitat: Open savannah and dense coastal forests
Food: Crickets, grasshoppers gleaned from branches and ground
Soc. Org: Gregarious - colonies

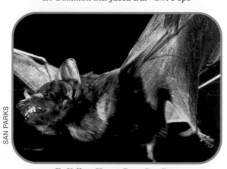

E: Yellow House Bat   Sw: Popo

Yellow House Bat *(Scotophilus dinganii)*
Sw: Popo

Length: 123 - 14mm
Weight: 22 - 37g
Litter: 1 - 3
Gestation: Not known
Active: Nocturnal

Habitat: Savannah woodlands, lower altitudes
Food: Aerial insect feeder, bugs, flies, moths
Soc. Org: Gregarious - up to 12

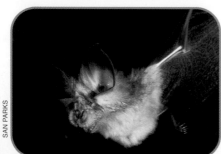

E: Darling's Horseshoe Bat   Sw: Popo

Darling's Horseshoe Bat *(Rhinolophus darlingi)*
Sw: Popo

Length: 80 - 90mm
Weight: 8 - 10g
Litter: 1 - 2
Gestation: Not known
Active: Nocturnal

Habitat: Savannah woodland, rocky terrain
Food: Insects
Soc. Org: Colonies of a few dozen

Hildebrandt's Horseshoe Bat *(Rhinolophus hildebrandtii)*
Sw: Popo

Length: 108 - 125mm
Weight: 26 - 32g
Litter: Not known
Gestation: Not known
Active: Nocturnal

Habitat: Savannah woodland
Food: Insects - aerial foragers in dense clutter
Soc. Org: Gregarious, colonies of a few hundred

E: Hildebrandt's Horseshoe Bat   Sw: Popo

Little Free-tailed Bat *(Chaerephon pumilis)*
Sw: Popo

Length: 70 - 120mm
Weight: 10 - 16g
Litter: One
Gestation: Not known
Active: Nocturnal

Habitat: Varied, savannah, mountains, arid
Food: Bugs, beetles, moths, aerial feeders
Soc. Org: Gregarious

E: Little Free-tailed Bat   Sw: Popo

Angolan Free-tailed Bat *(Mops condylurus)*
Sw: Popo

Length: 110 - 125mm
Weight: 16 - 22g
Litter: One
Gestation: 58 days
Active: Nocturnal

Habitat: Varied, not in deserts
Food: Beetles, high aerial feeders (strong jaws)
Soc. Org: Gregarious

E: Angolan Free-tailed Bat   Sw: Popo

Schlieffen's Bat *(Nycticeius schlieffeni)*
Sw: Popo

Length: 65 - 80mm
Weight: 3,7 - 5,0g
Litter: 1 - 3
Gestation: 11 weeks
Active: Nocturnal

Habitat: Savannah woodland, riparian, near pans
Food: Beetles, lacewings, flies, moths, bugs
Soc. Org: Solitary

E: Schlieffen's Bat   Sw: Popo

ANIMALS – MAMMALS

129

Lion

REPTILES AND AMPHIBIANS

Agama Lizard (Agama agama)

REPTILES AND AMPHIBIANS

INTRODUCTION TO REPTILES

This section will provide just a few photographic examples of the main groups of reptiles to give an understanding of the group as a whole. Hopefully it will also stimulate an interest in this fascinating group regarded by most people as 'less than charming'.

The most obvious characteristic of reptiles is their dry, horny skin that is usually modified into scales. The scales prevent water loss through the skin. Other differences to mammals is that they have a single occipital condyle (knob at the back of the skull) where mammals have two. They have a single bone in the ear, instead of the three found in mammals. Unlike mammals, each half of the lower jaw consists of several bones. Reptiles are cold-blooded. This term is confusing since their blood temperature is often higher than that of mammals. 'Cold-blooded' simply means that they obtain their heat externally, mostly from the sun. They regulate their body temperature by moving between sun and shade, in many cases from above ground to under ground. Mammals generate their heat internally by metabolising food. Reptiles have the ability to become temporarily dormant during cold weather and can survive and grow on much less food than mammals.

The first reptiles occurred about 315 million years ago and for about 150 million years the dinosaurs and their relatives dominated the earth, more specifically during the Jurassic era between 190 million to 130 million years ago (Branch, 1996).

Snake check list

Snakes probably evolved from legless lizards. Their eyes lack eyelids, they have no external ears, the tongue is retractile and can be withdrawn into a sheath. They have long backbones of up to 440 vertebrae and many ribs that are used for locomotion and to maintain body shape. They are all carnivorous. In many species the lower jaw can be dislocated to swallow large prey. They regularly shed their skin, usually in one piece, starting at the nose (Bill Branch, 1996). Only a few species of snake can shed their tail but they do not have the ability to regenerate a new one.

Mozambique Spitting Cobra (Naje mossambica)

African Rock Python (Python sebae)

SAN PARKS

SAN PARKS

Black Mamba (Dendroaspis polylepus)

Egyptian Cobra (Naje haje)

Puff Adder (Bitis arietans)

Rhombic Night Adder (Causus rhombeatus)

Tree Snake or Boomslang (Dispholidus typus)

Spotted Bush Snake (Philothamnus semivariegatus)

Shield-nosed Snake (Aspidelaps scutatus)

Sand Snake (Psammophis sp.)

REPTILES AND AMPHIBIANS

REPTILES AND AMPHIBIANS

VENOMOUS SNAKES OF TANZANIA

Venomous Snakes of Africa Of the ±2 000 species of snakes found in the world, only 300 are dangerous to man and very few will attack if not threatened. Of these, about 50 are marine

African Rock Python

and therefore seldom encountered. Only 14 African snakes have been recorded to have caused deaths. They are the Puff Adder, the Gaboon Adder, the Black Mamba, the Green Mamba, the five Cobras (Cape Cobra, Egyptian Cobra, Mozambique Spitting Cobra, Black Spitting Cobra and the Western Barred Cobra), the Namibian Coral Snake, the Rinkhals, the Boomslang, the Bird Snake and the African Rock Python. The Rock Python is not poisonous but kills by constricting and swallowing its prey whole.

The number of snakebite deaths are insignificant compared to other causes of death. People are generally terrified of snakes but snakes will only attack when cornered. They occupy a vital niche in the food chain and are extremely important in vermin control as they feed mainly on rodents.

Snake venom: Snake venom is produced by the salivary glands and has evolved from normal digestive enzymes, not unlike the enzymes found in human saliva. In venomous snakes the salivary gland has been modified to form a venom gland, which is called Duvernoy's gland in some groups. A complex muscle and duct system causes venom to ooze into the hollow, syringe-like fangs on voluntary contraction. The amount of venom injected is pre-determined and depends on the size of prey or how threatened a snake feels.

Fangs: Fang replacement occurs at intervals throughout the life of the snake. The poisonous snakes can be divided into front-fanged and back-fanged snakes. The venom of front-fanged snakes is cytotoxic, which means it affects the body tissue (Adders), and neurotoxic, which means it affects the nervous system (Mambas and Cobras). The venom of back-fanged snakes affects the blood circulation by preventing blood-clotting (Tree Snake/Boomslang and Vine Snake). The following snakes occuring in Tanzania are considered deadly: The Black Mamba, the Puff Adder, the Night Adder, the Egyptian Cobra, the Mozambique Spitting Cobra, the Tree Snake and the Vine Snake.

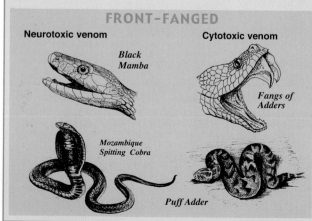

FRONT-FANGED

Neurotoxic venom

Black Mamba

Cytotoxic venom

Fangs of Adders

Mozambique Spitting Cobra

Puff Adder

BACK-FANGED

Venom prevents blood-clotting

Tree Snake

Vine Snake

Lizards differ from snakes in that they have moveable eyelids, external ears and the two halves of the lower jaw are fused. Many Lizards and Skinks can shed their tails and regrow new ones. The most common lizard-like reptiles we encounter in Africa are the Monitor Lizards, Lizards, Skinks, Geckos, Agama Lizards and the Chameleons.

Nile or Water Monitor (Varanus niloticus)

Nile or Water Monitor (Varanus niloticus)

Flap-necked Chameleon (Chamaeleo dilepis)

Flap-necked Chameleon (Chamaeleo dilepis)

Rock Agama (Agama agama)

Common Flat Lizard (Platysaurus intermedius)

Gecko (Pachydactylus sp.)

Striped Sandveld Lizard (Nucras tessellata)

REPTILES AND AMPHIBIANS

135

REPTILES AND AMPHIBIANS

The first tortoises date back about 210 million years. The Tortoise has both a skeleton and a protective, horny shell. The horny shell is attached to a bony case which in turn is fused to the rib cage. The peculiar result is that the shoulder blades and hip bones are situated within the rib cage. They all lay eggs and incubation can take anything from 4 to 15 months. There is a distinction between tortoises and terrapins. Tortoises are terrestrial and terrapins are semi-aquatic in fresh water. Turtles are found only in the ocean.

Tortoises eat mainly grass and forbs (small herbs) whereas terrapins are carnivorous. Terrapins submerge themselves at the water's edge and catch birds up to the size of doves, as they come down to drink.

Parrot-beaked Tortoise (Homopus areolatus)

Leopard Tortoise (Geochelone pardalis)

Angulate Tortoise (Chersina angulata)

Tent Tortoise (Pysammobates tentorius)

Hinged Tortoise (Kinikye sp.)

Serated Terrapin (Pelusios subniger)

INTERESTING FACTS ABOUT AMPHIBIANS

Like reptiles, amphibians are ectothermic vertebrates, which means that they depend on outside heat sources rather than metabolic heat. In general, they are referred to as cold-blooded, but like with reptiles, this is a confusing term as their blood is not cold.

Feeding Frogs and toads are carnivorous, feeding mainly on insects. They have large gapes and their tongues are essential feeding tools as they are sticky and used to transfer food to the mouth. The teeth are reduced or absent in some genera, as they mainly use them to restrain prey. The bullfrog has large projections on the lower jaw which serve the function of teeth.

Calls Only adult males produce calls during the breeding season, as they attract females that are ready to mate by means of sound, not vision or smell. Calling often intensifies after heavy rainstorms. There are always more males ready to mate than females. A female usually only mates once or twice in a season while a male mates repeatedly.

Sound is produced by inflating the lungs and shifting the air from the lungs to the buccal cavity, causing the vocal cords of the larynx to vibrate. The sound is intensified by resonance in a thin-walled extension of the buccal cavity - the vocal sack. The air is shunted back and forth to produce repeated calls.

Mating The female advertisers her availability by approaching the male closely, after which clasping will ensue. The correct term for clasping is 'amplexus'. Fertilisation is external and therefore the male does not have a sexual organ to insert spermatozoa into the female. There are three kinds of clasping - under the forearms, clasping around the waist and an unusual kind employed by rainfrogs, where the male adheres to the female, literally because the arms are to short to clasp.

Amplexus usually only lasts about 30 minutes but may last a few weeks in some species. After clasping, the male prods the flanks of the female with his forearms. The male is always smaller than the female, causing the two cloacae to be very close during egg-laying. As the eggs are ejected the ejaculation of siminal fluid by the male follows. The sequence is repeated several times. Some toads may lay up to 20 000 eggs but the rain frogs only lay 25 to 50 eggs.

The eggs The eggs are only about 1mm to 2mm in diameter. In the female's body they are covered by a jelly-like secretion. This causes the eggs to form clusters or strings. Tree Frogs 'whip up' the eggs into a stiff foam which is suspended on branches over water - a familiar sight in the bush. The foam forms a hard protective crust to prevent dehydration of the eggs. As the tadpoles are ready to hatch, they become heavy and the foam nest breaks open into the water.

Metamorphosis
Amphibian development involves metamorphosis in which the larva takes on a fish-like shape called a tadpole. In puddle-breeding species the larval or tadpole life may be just a few short weeks but with species that breed in permanent water it may be as long as nine months or even more. The tadpole stage of Rain Frogs, which burrow, take place underground within a jelly encasement. Metamorphosis involves both physical and physiological changes. They loose their tails, gills, larval mouth and develop a tympanum, eyelids, tongue and a cornified skin. They change from ammonia excretion to urea excretion and from being herbivorous to being carnivorous.

Metamorphosis (tadpole to frog/toad)

Bullfrog (Pyxicephalus adspersus)

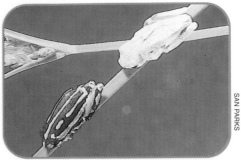

Painted Reed Frog (Hyperolius marmoratus)

Banded Rubber Frog (Phrynomantis bifasciatus)

Clawless Frog (Xenopus laevis)

Toad (Bufo sp.)

Rain Frog (Breviceps sp.)

Snoring Puddle Frog (Phrynobatrachus natalensis)

River Frog (Rana sp.)

REPTILES AND AMPHIBIANS

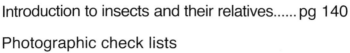

INSECTS

INSECTS AND RELATIVES

Milkweed Locust (Phymateus morbillosus)

INTRODUCTION TO INSECTS

Insects and their relatives Insects belong to a group of organisms that have three pairs of legs, a single pair of antennae and a body divided into three sections - a head, thorax and abdomen. Other closely-related, insect-like creatures which do not fulfil the above requirements are spiders, harvestmen, sunspiders, scorpions, whipscorpions, ticks, mites, centipedes, millipedes and crustaceans.

Spider

Number of insect species Insects are by far the most numerous group of organisms on earth. Only a fraction of them have been named and described - and that accounts for about one million species. Compare this with ±260 000 described plant species and only 50 000 vertebrates. It is estimated that there may be as many as 6 million insect species in the world.

Economic value of insects Insects have a tremendous influence on our lives and on the ecology - both positive and negative. Just think of the enormous role they play in pollination of economic crops, not to mention pollination of natural plants. Some insects, like Dung Beetles, play a very important role in returning nutrients to the soil by means of the dung balls they bury. Insects form an important part of the food chain, providing a source of food to countless invertebrates, birds, reptiles, amphibians, small mammals and even larger mammals such as the Aardvark, Aardwolf, the Bat-eared Fox and the Pangolin.

Disease Insects can also cause death on an epidemic scale. A good example is that of the 'black death' during the 14th century, which caused 75 million deaths and was spread by means of rat fleas. Mosquitos cause about 2 million deaths annually as they are the carriers of the parasite that causes malaria. Only the female Mosquito sucks blood and is therefore responsible for transmitting the disease. She holds her body at a 45° angle whilst sucking.

The female Malaria mosquito

Impact on pastures Very few people realise the effect of termites on natural grazing - they have the ability to destroy about 70% of grazing in natural veld. Locusts have caused the devastation of entire crops in the past.

Locust

Life history of insects The life history of insects can follow two patterns - the first is where the eggs hatch into nymphs that resemble the adult, except that they are wingless. They become adults after several moults. The other pattern involves the eggs hatching into a caterpillar after which it enters a pupal stage and only then adulthood. This pattern allows for the caterpillar to feed and grow to a size similar to that of the adult.

Flightless Dung Beetles gathering dung

Pangolins control the numbers of ants and termites by feeding on them

Butterflies

Common Diadem - female
(Hypolimnas misippus)

Common Diadem - male
(Hypolimnas misippus)

Blue Pansy
(Junonia oenone)

Guinea Fowl
(Hamanumida daedalus)

Grass Yellow
(Eurema sp.)

Dotted Border
(Mylothris agathine)

Painted Lady
(Vanessa cardui)

Brown-veined White
(Belenois aurota aurota)

Queen Purple Tip
(Colotis regina)

Foxy Charaxes - upper side
(Charaxes candiope)

Foxy Charaxes - underside
(Charaxes candiope)

Bushveld Charaxes
(Charaxes achaemenes)

African Monarch
(Danaus chrysippus)

Citrus Swallowtail
(Papilio demodocus)

Scarlet Tip
(Colotis danae)

INSECTS AND RELATIVES

141

INSECTS AND RELATIVES

Moths check list

Mopane Moth
(Gonimbrasia belina)

Mopane Moth
(Gonimbrasia belina)

Beautiful Tiger
(Amphicallia bellatrix)

Irian Emperor
(Pseudobunaea irius)

Speckled Emperor
(Gynanisa maia)

Arrow Sphinx
(Lophostethus dumolinii)

Emperor Moth
(Bunaea alcinae)

Common Nephele
(Nephele comma)

Southern Atlas
(Epiphora bauhiniae)

Locusts and grasshoppers check list

Common Milkweed Locust
(Phymateus morbillosus)

Green Milkweed Locust
(Phymateus viridipes)

Elegant Grasshopper
(Zonocerus elegans)

142

Two-spotted Ground Beetle
(Thermophilum homoplatum)

Fruit Chafer
(Dicranorrhina derbyana)

Net-winged Beetle
(Lycus melanurus)

Yellow-edge Water Beetle
(Hydaticus bivittatus)

Blister Beetle or CMR Beetle
(Mylabris oculata)

Blister Beetle or CMR Beetle
(Mylabris sp.)

Giant Jewel Beetle
(Sternocera orissa)

Striped Toktokkie Beetle
(Psammodus striatus)

Rounded Toktokkie Beetle
(Moluris pseudonitida)

Giant Longhorn Beetle
(Acanthophorus palmata)

Flightless Dung Beetle
(Circellium bacchus)

Eucalypt Borer or Phoracantha
Longhorn Beetle (Phoracantha recurva)

Giant Assassin Bug
(Platymeris sp.)

Assassin Bug
(Pantoleistes sp.)

Christmas Beetle

INSECTS AND RELATIVES

143

Other Insects

INSECTS AND RELATIVES

Hippo Fly
(Tabanus biguttatus)

Elephant Fly
(Philoliche sp.)

Carpenter Bee
(Xylocopa caffra)

Blowfly
(Family hippoboscidae)

Antlion
(Family myrmeleontidae)

Groundling
(Brachythemis sp.)

Honey Bee
(Apis mellifera)

Corn Cricket
(Hetrodus pupus)

Wasp
(Anterhynchium natalense)

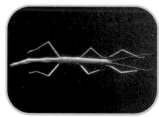

Indian Stick Insect
(Phymateus sp.)

Water Scorpion
(Laccotrephes sp.)

Drop-tail Ants
(Myrmicaria natalensis)

Male Driver Ant
(Dorylus helvolus)

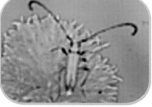

Common Metallic Longhorn
(Promeces sp.)

Velvet Ant
(Dolichomutilla sp.)

144

Scorpions and Solifuges

SCORPIONS AND SOLIFUGES CHECK LIST

Family Buthidae

Family Scorpionidae

Solifuge

SCORPIONS

Scorpions are represented by mainly two families in Africa, the *Scorpiondae* and the *Buthidae*. All scorpions are poisonous, but only the *Buthidae* are dangerous and, in certain cases, lethal to man. How do we distinguish the *Buthidae* from the relatively harmless *Scorpiondae*? An easy general rule is to look at the 'pincers', the correct technical term being 'pedipalps'. Scorpions with small pedipalps and large tails are very poisonous (*Buthidae*) and those with large pedipalps and reduced tails are less poisonous (*Scorpiondae*). The only three genera worth mentioning as regards their poison are *Parabuthus* spp., *Buthotus* spp. and *Uroplectes* spp., all belonging to the family *Buthidae*.

Buthidae:
Note the thick tail and reduced pedipalps

Scorpions are ovoviviparous, which means that the eggs are bred within the female reproductive tract and the young are born alive. The development takes several months or even a year, with as many as 90 young produced in some cases. They are small replicas (only a few millimetres) of the adult, but almost white in

Scorpionidae:
Note the thin tail and the large pedipapls

colour. They immediately climb on the mother's back and not even the most anxious 'scorpiophobic' can deny the cuteness of this sight! Their courtship is also unique, very lengthy and rather romantic. The male gently grabs the female with his pedipalps and then proceeds to 'dance' with her for hours on end - in fact, it sometimes lasts for days. Eventually he deposits a spermatophore (sperm-bearing vesicle), which is attached to the ground. A wing-like lever extends from the spermatophore which, if touched, will release the sperms.

Female carrying young

The male then carefully manoeuvres the female so that her genital area touches the lever for the sperm to be released into the female orifice. Scorpions have an exceptionally long life-span, taking a few years to grow to maturity. It was reported that a species of *Parabuthus villosus* was kept alive in a laboratory for more than a year without food or water!

Mating dance

145

Spider check list

Orb-web Spider nest

Garden Orb-web Spider
(Argiope australis)

Buckspoor Spider nest
(Seothyra sp.)

Baboon Spider
(Family Theraphosidae)

Baboon Spider
(Family Theraphosidae)

Kite Spider
(Gasteracantha milvoides)

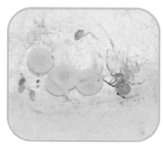

Widow Spider
(Latrodectus sp.)

Banded-legged Golden Orb-web Spider
(Nephila senegalensis)

Orb-web Spider carrying eggs
(Nephila senegalensis)

GASTROPODS – SNAILS

Snail

Snails are not Arthropods like insects, they are Gastropods, which means 'stomach foot' because they slide along their stomachs. As they crawl they ooze a trail of slime to ease their way over the ground. They feed on plants and can become pests in the garden. Fresh water snails are preyed upon by the Open-billed Stork, which has a specially adapted open bill to crush the shell.

INSECTS AND RELATIVES

BIRDS

Greater Flamingo

BIRD SPECIES OF THE NCA

More than 550 bird species have been recorded in the NCA, of which some are resident and some migratory. Because of the variety of habitat types, from montane forest, to dry bush, to grasslands and salt lakes, the diversity of birds is spectacular. Many water birds are attracted by salt lakes and the variety and numbers at Lake Magadi in the Ngorongoro Crater and Lake Ndutu are very high. Many fruit-eating birds, like the Turacos and the Hornbills, occur in the forests. The highlands are also particularly rich in sunbirds.

The Augur Buzzard is the most common raptor in the highlands whilst in the open plains, the Eastern Pale Chanting Goshawk and the Montagu's Harrier are the most common. The Rueppell's Griffon has an important breeding site at Ilkarian Gorge in the NCA - one of only a handful of sites left in Africa. It is also one of the largest nesting sites, consisting of about 2 000 breeding pairs. The Fischer's Lovebird is endemic to northern Tanzania and so is the commonly seen Rufous-tailed Weaver.

Quick alphabetical reference to the bird groups

Take note: The numbers refer to the group numbers in the bird checklist:

BIRDS

Quick alphabetical reference to the bird groups

BIRDS

Bird check list

1   Ostrich

Ostrich ☐

An Ostrich egg contains the equivalent of two dozen hens' eggs. The male, with its black feathers, incubates at night and the grey-brown female during the day. An adult male stands over 2,5m tall and weighs about 160kg.

Ostrich

2   Pelicans

Great White Pelican ☐

Pink-backed Pelican ☐

The Pelican has a dispensable pouch under its lower mandible which is used to scoop up fish. They form joint fishing parties, herding and cornering the fish. They cannot fly with fish in the pouch, as it will upset their centre of gravity. Fish for nestlings is swallowed and later regurgitated. The chick inserts its head into the adult's gullet to get its food. The White Pelican nests on the ground while the Pink-backed Pelican nests in trees. They do round trips of up to 200km per day for food.

Great White Pelican

Pink-backed Pelican

3   Storks

Abdim's Stork ☐

African Open-billed Stork ☐

Black Stork ☐

Marabou Stork ☐

Saddle-billed Stork ☐

White Stork ☐

Whoolly-necked Stork ☐

Yellow-billed Stork ☐

The Open-billed Stork has a gap between its mandibles to enable it to grasp and crush the snails on which it feeds.

Abdim's Stork

African Open-billed Stork

Marabou Stork

Saddle-billed Stork

Woolly Necked Stork

Yellow-billed Stork

The Saddle-billed Stork is the largest stork at 1,3m tall.   The Marabou Stork has no feathers on its head and neck - an adaptation to feed on carrion, but it also eats fish, especially marooned Barbel.

Herons   4

Black-headed Heron ☐

Black Heron ☐

Green-backed Heron ☐

Madagascar Squacco Heron ☐

Scuacco Heron ☐

Black-crowned Night Heron ☐

Goliath Heron ☐

Grey Heron ☐

Purple Heron ☐

Rufous-bellied Heron ☐

Black-headed Heron

Green-backed Heron

Squacco Heron

Grey Heron

Bird check list

Black Heron

Purple Heron

Goliath Heron

Rufous-bellied Heron

5 Egrets

Great White Egret

Great White Egret ☐

Cattle Egret ☐

Yellow-billed Egret ☐

Little Egret ☐

Cattle Egret

The Great White Egret is the largest Egret with a distinct 'kink' in its neck, black legs and a yellow bill, which turns black during breeding. The Yellow-billed Egret always has a yellow bill, black legs with yellow thighs. The Little Egret has a black bill, black legs with yellow feet.

Yellow-billed Egret

Little Egret

6 Grebes / Dabchicks

Little Grebe / Dabchick

Little Grebe / Dabchick ☐

Black-necked Grebe ☐

Great Crested Grebe ☐

Dabchicks dive for frogs and tadpoles to eat.

Darters 7

African Darter

African Darter ☐

The African Darter uses its bill like a spear, diving at great speed and spearing its prey. They lack the protective oil layer on their feathers and thus need to dry their wings in the sun.

Cormorants 8

Long-tailed Cormorant

Great Cormorant ☐

Long-tailed Cormorant ☐

Cormorants dive under water to catch fish. The lack of oil on their feathers enables them to dive deeper but they cannot float like other water birds.

Bitterns 9

The Dwarf Bittern is an 'opportunistic breeder', favouring areas that are seasonally flooded.

Little Bittern ☐

Dwarf Bittern ☐

Hamerkops 10

Hamerkop

Hamerkop ☐

Hamerkops build huge nests of up to 1,5m in diameter that can weigh up to 50kg or more. Inside is a tunnel and chamber which are plastered with mud. They collect all kinds of objects such as plastic, metal and bones to decorate the nest.

Ibises 11

Sacred Ibis

Sacred Ibis ☐

Hadada Ibis ☐

Glossy Ibis ☐

The Hadada Ibis mates for life. They are grassland birds, foraging on the ground.

BIRDS

151

BIRDS

Hadada Ibis

Glossy Ibis

12 Flamingos

Greater Flamingo ☐

Lesser Flamingo ☐

Greater Flamingo

Flamingos are filter feeders and feed almost exclusively on plankton - microscopic plants and animals that occur in mud and on the surface of shallow, saline lakes. The bill is sharply recurved and they invert their bill when feeding, using the tongue to pump the water through the filtering lamellae which allow only the plankton through. Lesser Flamingos select mainly for blue-green algae such as *Saliginella* and diatoms.

Lesser Flamingo

13 Spoonbills

African Spoonbill ☐

Spoonbills feed by moving their slightly open, spatulate bill from side to side and taking in waterborne organisms, even small fish. They breed in Africa and roost communally, often on partially submerged trees.

African Spoonbill

14 Ducks

African Black Duck ☐

Fulvous Whistling Duck ☐

Knob-billed Duck ☐

Tufted Duck ☐

White-backed Duck ☐

Knob-billed Duck

There are no fish-eating ducks in Africa.

White-faced Whistling Duck ☐

Yellow-billed duck ☐

White-faced Whistling Duck

Yellow-billed Duck

Garganeys 15

Garganey ☐

Pintails 16

Northern Pintail ☐

Pochards 17

Southern Pochard ☐

Shoveller 18

Northern Shoveller ☐

Teals 19

Cape Teal ☐

Hottentot Teal ☐

Red-billed Teal ☐

Cape Teal

The Red-billed Teal is a wanderer, covering distances of 1 600km per year.

Hottentot Teal

Red-billed Teal

Wigeons 20

Eurasian Wigeon ☐

Bird check list

21 Geese

African Pygmy Goose ☐
Egyptian Goose ☐
Spur-winged Goose ☐

Although they are called Geese, there are no true geese in Africa south of the Sahara.

African Pygmy Goose

Egyptian Goose   *Spur-winged Goose*

22 Jacanas

African Jacana ☐

African Jacanas have a polyandrous mating system - that is where the females mate, lay the eggs and leave the male to raise the chicks. She may even destroy another male's eggs to get him to mate with her.

African Jacana

23 Water Rails

African Water Rail ☐

24 Crakes

Black Crake ☐
African Crake ☐
Corncrake ☐

The Black Crake feeds on small mollusks, crustaceans, insects, even small birds and eggs.

Black Crake

25 Gallinules/Swamphens

Purple Swamphen (Gallinule) ☐
Allen's Gallinule ☐

Moorhens 26

Common Moorhen ☐
Lesser Moorhen ☐

Moorhens feed on aquatic plants and animals and their nests consist of 'bowls' of reeds which they build in shallow water.

Common Moorhen

Coots 27

Coots are monogamous.

Red-knobbed Coot ☐

Avocets 28

Avocets prefer pans in semi-arid areas.

Eurasian Avocet ☐

Stilts 29

Common Stilt ☐

The Stilt has the longest legs in comparison with its body of any bird. Their nests are almost always surrounded by shallow water and consist of piled-up plant material. They frequently mob potential predators.

Common Stilt

Thicknees 30

Water Thicknee ☐
Spotted Thicknee ☐

The large eyes of Thicknees indicate that they are semi-nocturnal, enabling them to see at night. The Water Thicknee is more diurnal. They both feed on insects, snails, frogs and crabs. The Water Thicknee even eats the shells of snails and crabs. Both have a characteristic whistle-like piping call, often heard at night. They both breed on the ground in shallow scrapes surrounded by pellets or animal droppings. The Water Thicknee usually nests closer to the water.

Water Thicknee

Spotted Thicknee

BIRDS

31 — Gulls

Grey-headed Gull

Black-headed Gull ☐
Grey-headed Gull ☐
Lesser Black-backed Gull ☐

The Grey-headed Gull is a scavenger and will also kill nestlings of other water birds.

32 — Terns

Whiskered Tern

Sandwich Tern ☐
Whiskered Tern ☐
White-winged Black Tern ☐

Terns feed by plucking from the surface or plunging into the water.

33 — Skimmers

African Skimmer

African Skimmer ☐

The Skimmer feeds by flying close to the water with its bill open, the lower mandible scything the surface for fish. They nest in deep scrapes in the ground. They favour brackish lakes.

34 — Coursers

Temminck's Courser ☐
Two-banded Courser ☐
Violet-tipped Courser ☐
Three-banded/Heuglin's Courser ☐

Temminck's Courser

Two-banded Courser   *Three-banded Courser*

Pratincoles — 35

Commom Pratincole

Common Pratincole ☐

Pratincoles are monogamous and they nest on floodplain mudflats, almost always near water. They lay the eggs on bare ground, often in a hoofprint. A predator is lured away by the adult feigning injury.

Plovers — 36

Kittlitz's Plover

Caspian Plover ☐
Little Ringed Plover ☐
Ringed Plover ☐
Kittlitz's Plover ☐
Three-banded Plover ☐
Chestnut-banded Plover ☐

Three-banded Plover   *Chestnut-banded Plover*

Lapwings — 37

African Wattled Lapwing

African Wattled Lapwing ☐
Blacksmith Lapwing ☐
Black-winged Lapwing ☐
Crowned Lapwing ☐
Senegal Lapwing ☐
Spur-winged Lapwing ☐
Long-toed Lapwing ☐

Blacksmith Lapwing   *Crowned Lapwing*

Senegal Lapwing   *Long-toed Lapwing*

38 Curlews

Curlews are waders, having long, curved bills.

Eurasian Curlew ☐

39 Greenshanks

Greenshank ☐

Greenshank

The Greenshank is very similar to the Marsh Sandpiper, the Greenshank having a thicker, slightly upward curving bill and light green legs. They both wade in deeper water than other waders.

40 Godwits

Godwits have very long bills and the body shape of a Lapwing.

Black-tailed Godwit ☐

41 Redshanks

The legs and base of bill of a Redshank are red. They are waders, living on aquatic life.

Redshank ☐

Spotted Redshank ☐

42 Ruffs

Ruff ☐

Ruff

Technically, the 'Ruff' is the male and the 'Reeve' is the female. Ruffs form large flocks. The male is much larger and their legs are orange. They breed in Europe and are summer migrants in Africa.

Sandpipers 43

Common Sandpiper

Buff-breasted Sandpiper ☐

Common Sandpiper ☐

Curlew Sandpiper ☐

Green Sandpiper ☐

Marsh Sandpiper ☐

Ruddy Sandpiper ☐

Terek Sandpiper ☐

Wood Sandpiper ☐

Curlew Sandpiper

Sandpipers often bob their heads whilst feeding - it is said to help with focusing on their underwater prey. They feed on small aquatic fauna.

Marsh Sandpiper   *Wood Sandpiper*

Stints 44

Little Stint ☐

Temminck's Stint ☐

The Little Stint breeds in Europe and Asia and is a summer visitor in Africa. They usually forage in flocks. Their food is mollusks, crustaceans, insects and worms.

Little Stint

Snipes 45

African Snipe ☐

Common Snipe ☐

Great Snipe ☐

Painted Snipe ☐

The Common Snipe is a migrant.

Common Snipe

BIRDS

BIRDS

The Common Snipe has a very long bill which it uses to probe for aquatic fauna. The Painted Snipe has a polyandrous mating system, like the Jacana. The female may mate and produce eggs with up to four males in one season.

Painted Snipe

46 Cranes

Grey-crowned Crane ☐

Crowned Cranes roost in flocks of 10-200, often on islands within rivers. They feed solitary or in pairs. They feed on insects, frogs, reptiles and grain, even grass seeds which they strip off the standing grass.

Grey-crowned Crane

47 Secretary Bird

Secretary Bird ☐

The Secretary Bird feeds mainly on snakes, frogs, lizards and rodents. They swallow their prey whole. They are so named because of the quills on their head, reminiscent of a secretary with a pen above his/her ear.

Secretary Bird

48 Eagles

African Fish Eagle ☐
African Hawk Eagle ☐
Ayres's Hawk Eagle ☐
Bateleur Eagle ☐
Booted Eagle ☐
Brown Snake Eagle ☐
Crowned Eagle ☐
Imperial Eagle ☐
Lesser-spotted Eagle ☐
Long-crested Eagle ☐

African Fish Eagle

African Hawk Eagle

Martial Eagle ☐
Short-toed Snake Eagle ☐
Tawny Eagle ☐
Verreaux's Eagle ☐
Wahlberg's Eagle ☐

Bateleur Eagle

Bateleur Eagle (immature)

Black-breasted Snake Eagle

Brown Snake Eagle

Martial Eagle

Tawny Eagle (light)

Tawny Eagle (dark)

Verreaux's Eagle

The eyes of birds of prey are positioned to the front of the head to provide them with binocular vision. All birds have colour vision. The vision of raptors is extremely good but their sense of smell is poor.

Osprey 49

Osprey ☐

Ospreys feed on fish, plunging into the water feet first, sometimes submerging completely. They carry the fish by the head to offer the least wind resistance and their feet are rough to ensure a tight grip.

Osprey

Bird check list

50   Vultures

African White-backed Vulture ☐

Egyptian Vulture ☐

Hooded Vulture ☐

Lammergeier ☐

Lappet-faced Vulture ☐

Palm-nut Vulture ☐

Rueppell's Griffon ☐

White-headed Vulture ☐

African White-backed Vulture

Hooded Vulture

Vultures feed on carrion. They have no feathers on their neck, enabling them to feed inside a carcass. Refer to pg 49 for more details.

Lammergeier

Lappet-faced Vulture

Rueppell's Griffon

White-headed Vulture

51   Harriers

African Marsh Harrier ☐

Eurasian Marsh Harrier ☐

Montagu's Harrier ☐

Pallid Harrier ☐

Montagu's Harriers are very common on the Serengeti Plains.

Montagu's Harrier

African Marsh Harriers are associated with marshy areas, particularly reedbeds. They fly with their heads looking down whilst hunting. The male brings its prey to the female. She flies off the nest and takes it in full flight by a swift upside-down manoeuvre. They feed on frogs, rodents and birds.

African Marsh Harrier

Goshawks   52

African Goshawk ☐

Black Goshawk ☐

Eastern Pale Chanting ☐

Dark Chanting Goshawk ☐

Eastern Goshawk ☐

Gabar Goshawk ☐

Eastern Pale Chanting Goshawk (male)

Eastern Pale Chanting Goshawk (female)

Dark Chanting Goshawk

Gabar Goshawk

Gabar Goshawk (melanistic)

Goshawks are called 'short-winged hawks' (as opposed to the long-winged falcons). The Goshawk hunts in wooded country, watching from a perch and making a quick dash. A Gabar Goshawk's nest can be recognised by the spider web that forms part of it. The birds have been observed carrying Communal Spiders (*Stegodyphus sp.*) to their nest early in the nest-building process. Various suggestions have been put forward, such as camouflage, strengthening and parasite control, possibly a combination of all three.

Bird check list

53   Buzzards

Augur Buzzard

Augur Buzzard ☐
Common Buzzard ☐
Grasshopper Buzzard ☐
Lizzard Buzzard ☐
Mountain Buzzard ☐
Western Honey-buzzard ☐

Augur Buzzard (melanistic)

The Augur Buzzard frequents mountains and kopjes and they often nest on rock ledges. The nest is about 40cm across and they line the nest with the lichen, Old Man's Beard (*Usnea sp.*), where available. They eat mainly snakes, lizards, insects and birds.

54   Kestrels

Common Kestrel

Common Kestrel ☐
Grey-eyed Kestrel ☐
Lesser Kestrel ☐
White-eyed Kestrel ☐

Lesser Kestrel

The Lesser Kestrel is a palaearctic migrant, that means they breed in Europe but come to Africa during the European winter. The Greater Kestrel breeds in Africa and uses deserted nests of raptors, varying in size from a Secretary Bird to a Black-shouldered Kite, preferring that of Pied Crows. Kestrels eat mainly insects but also small rodents and birds.

55   Falcons

Lanner Falcon

African Pygmy Falcon ☐
Eastern Red-footed Falcon ☐
Lanner Falcon ☐
Peregrine Falcon ☐
Red-necked Falcon ☐

Lanner Falcon (juvenile)

Falcons strike at great speed and force from above, often killing their prey on impact. In East Africa, Pygmy Falcons nest in a chamber of the communal nests of Sociable Weavers. A falcon's nest can be recognised by the ring of white droppings at the entrance.

Hawks   56

Hawks are short-winged and falcons long-winged. The Bat Hawk emerges at dusk and preys on bats, swifts and other late-flying birds. It swallows its prey whole in flight.

African Cuckoo-hawk ☐
African Harrier-hawk ☐
African Little Sparrow-hawk ☐
Bat Hawk ☐
Ovambo Sparrow-hawk ☐

Shikras   57

A Shikra is a hawk with red eyes.

Shikra ☐

Hobbies   58

Hobbies are actually just falcons, belonging to the same genus '*Falco*'.

African Hobbie ☐
Northern Hobbie ☐

Kites   59

Black Kite

Black Kite ☐
Black-shouldered Kite ☐

Black-shouldered Kite

The Black Kite can be recognised by its forked tail. It mainly scavenges, often ocurring at picnic sites. The Black-shouldered Kite is nomadic and roosts communally. Individuals are highly territorial. A female chooses the male with the best territory but she does not form a permanent bond with him. They do not have a distinct breeding season. It has been suggested that reproductive steroids in their rodent prey may trigger hormonal activity. They may raise a number of broods in one season.

60 Francolins

Coqui Francolin ☐
Crested Francolin ☐
Hildebrandt's Francolin ☐
Shelley's Francolin ☐

Coqui Francolin

Francolins have highly developed gizzards consisting of a corrugated, leathery lining surrounded by muscular walls. It contracts rhythmically whilst strong enzymes are secreted to aid breakdown of the grain they swallow whole. They occur in family groups and feed on seeds, berries, insects and other invertebrates.

Crested Francolin

61 Spurfowl

Grey-breasted Spurfowl ☐
Red-necked Spurfowl ☐
Yellow-fronted Spurfowl ☐

The Yellow-fronted Spurfowl and the Grey-breasted Spurfowl often interbreed in the Serengeti area.

Yellow-fronted Spurfowl

62 Guineafowl

Helmeted Guineafowl ☐

Guineafowls are monogamous. They form flocks during the non-breeding season, forming pairs in early summer to breed solitary. They often nest within a few hundred metres of each other.

Helmeted Guineafowl

63 Quails

Blue Quail ☐
Common Quail ☐

Quails are rainy season migrants. The Common Quail prefers grassland and fallow lands but the Blue Quail prefers margins of seasonally waterlogged areas.

Common Quail

64 Bustards

Black-bellied Bustard ☐
Buff-crested Bustard ☐
Denham's Bustard ☐
Hartlaub's Bustard ☐
Kori Bustard ☐
White-bellied Bustard ☐

Black-bellied Bustard

White-bellied Bustard

Bustards are ground birds and they nest on the ground. They are well camouflaged but the males have very visual mating displays, inflating their gular pouches and puffing out their neck feathers. This may attract several females. The males will mate with more than one female and that is where their duty ends. They do not help with raising the chicks. The Kori Bustard is the heaviest flying bird in Africa.

Kori Bustard

65 Sandgrouse

Black-faced Sandgrouse ☐
Chestnut-bellied Sandgrouse ☐
Yellow-throated Sandgrouse ☐

Sandgrouse occur in arid environments.

Yellow-throated Sandgrouse

66 Pigeons

African Green Pigeon ☐
Olive Pigeon ☐
Speckled Pigeon ☐

African Green Pigeon

Nestlings are fed by mouth on 'pigeon's milk', very similar in substance to milk produced by mammals.

Speckled Pigeon

BIRDS

159

Bird check list

67 Doves

African Mourning Dove

African Mourning Dove ☐
Dusky Turtle Dove ☐
Emerald-spotted Wood Dove ☐
Laughing Dove ☐

Doves feed mainly on seeds, occasionally insects.

Dusky Turtle Dove

Emerald-spotted Wood Dove

Laughing Dove

Ring-necked Dove

68 Lovebirds

Fischer's Lovebird

Fischer's Lovebird ☐
Yellow-collared Lovebird ☐

The Fischers Lovebird is endemic to northern Tanzania. Their numbers have been depleted because of the overseas bird trade.

69 Parrots

Brown Parrot

African Orange-bellied Parrot ☐
Brown Parrot ☐
Red-fronted Parrot ☐

Parrots eat mainly fruit.

Go-away Birds 70

Bare-faced Go-away Bird

Bare-faced Go-away Bird ☐
White-bellied Go-away Bird ☐

Go-away Birds have a characteristic 'kwe' sounding call. Hunters believe they warn game to 'go away', hence the name 'Go-away Bird'. They have strong, curved bills which enable them to cope with tough fruit husks. They depend on the fruit of indigenous trees but do feed insects to their young. They are very agile in trees, moving with a light, springy action. They have a semi-zygodactylous toe formation in which the outer toe protrudes at right angles to the foot and is free to move backward or forward.

White-bellied Go-away Bird

Turacos 71

Turacos are colourful forest birds. Parents feed the chicks by regurgitating undigested berries. The chicks do not pass faecal sacs and therefore the adult pecks at the anus and eats the liquid excreta.

Green Turaco ☐
Puple-crested Turaco ☐
Ross's Turaco ☐

Cuckoos 72

Great Spotted Cuckoo

African Cuckoo ☐
African Emerald Cuckoo ☐
Black-and-white Cuckoo ☐
Black Cuckoo ☐
Diederik's Cuckoo ☐
Eurasian Cuckoo ☐
Great Spotted Cuckoo ☐
Klaas's Cuckoo ☐
Lesser Cuckoo ☐
Levaillant's Cuckoo ☐
Red-chested Cuckoo ☐

Great Spotted Cuckoo

Bird check list

73 Coucals

Black Coucal ☐

White-browed Coucal ☐

Black Coucal

White-browed Coucal

Coucals are also called 'Bottle Birds' because their call resembles water bubbling out of a bottle. They are closely related to cuckoos but do not display parasitic behaviour. Most species are monogamous, except for the Black Coucal which can also be polyandrous (where a female mates and raises chicks with more than one male). Their eyes only open after ±5 days. Chicks defend themselves by hissing like a snake and by voiding nauseating liquid faeces (different to the encapsulated faecal sack that they normally produce).

74 Mousebirds

Blue-naped Mousebird ☐

Speckled Mousebird ☐

Speckled Mousebird

Mousebirds have the ability to turn their outer toes forwards or backwards, enabling them to creep along branches like mice. They often hang upside down and are even known to sleep like that.

75 Owls

African Grass Owl ☐

African Marsh Owl ☐

African Wood Owl ☐

Barn Owl ☐

Common Scops Owl ☐

African Marsh Owl

Pearl-spotted Owlet ☐

Spotted Eagle-owl ☐

Verreaux's Eagle-owl ☐

White-faced Scops Owl ☐

Owls can turn their heads through 270° and have superior night vision.

African Wood Owl

Barn Owl

Common Scops Owl

White-faced Scops Owl

Pearl-spotted Owlet

Spotted Eagle-owl

Verreaux's Eagle-owl

Nightjars 76

Dusky Nightjar ☐

Eurasian Nightjar ☐

Gabon Nightjar ☐

Slender-tailed Nightjar ☐

Pennant-wing Nighjar ☐

Nightjar

Swifts 77

Swifts feed, mate and collect nesting material on the wing. The European Swift remains airborne for 9 months of the year, only using a nest during breeding. It even sleeps in the air by ascending to great heights where its metabolism drops and it goes into a state of semi-sleep.

African Black Swift ☐

African Palm Swift ☐

Eurasian Swift ☐

Little Swift ☐

Mottled Swift ☐

Nyanza Swift ☐

Scarce Swift ☐

Bird check list

78 Spinetails

They are often associated with Baobab Trees. Their nests are vertical on branches.

Mottled Spinetail	☐

79 Kingfishers

Brown-hooded Kingfisher

Giant Kingfisher

African Pygmy Kingfisher ☐
Brown-hooded Kingfisher ☐
Giant Kingfisher ☐
Grey-headed Kingfisher ☐
Half-collared Kingfisher ☐
Malachite Kingfisher ☐
Pied Kingfisher ☐
Striped Kingfisher ☐
Woodland Kingfisher ☐

Not all Kingfishers eat fish, some eat insects.

Grey-headed Kingfisher

Half-collared Kingfisher

Malachite Kingfisher

Pied Kingfisher

Striped Kingfisher

Woodland Kingfisher

Trogons 80

Trogons are bright in colour and prefer riverine forest and dense woodland.

Bar-tailed Trogon ☐
Nerina's Trogon ☐

Bee-eaters 81

Blue-cheecked Bee-eater

Blue-cheeked Bee-eater ☐
Cinnamon-chested Bee-eater ☐
Eurasian Bee-eater ☐
Little Bee-eater ☐
Olive Bee-eater ☐
Swallow-tailed Bee-eater ☐
White-throated Bee-eater ☐

Eurasian Bee-eater

Bee-eaters use their long, curved bills to dig their nesting tunnels in earth embankments, using their feet as shovels.

Swallow-tailed Bee-eater

White-throated Bee-eater

Rollers 82

Broad-billed Roller

Broad-billed Roller ☐
Eurasian Roller ☐
Lilac-breasted Roller ☐
Rufous-crowned Roller ☐

'Roller' refers to their flight display.

Lilac-breasted Roller

Eurasian Roller

83   Hoopoes

African Hoopoe ☐

Green Wood Hoopoe ☐

African Hoopoe

Green Wood Hoopoe

The African Hoopoe utters a melodious hoop-hoop call but Green Wood Hoopoes travel in groups and are very noisy, sounding like a group of women laughing, as many of their African names indicate. The African Hoopoe often has two or three broods in the same season. It is referred to in the Old Testament as regards its poor nest sanitation. Their long bills enable them to probe under bark and in grass roots for invertebrates.

84   Scimitarbills

Scimitarbills are Wood Hoopoes have prominently curved bills.

Abyssinian Scimitarbill ☐

Scimitarbill ☐

85   Hornbills

African Grey Hornbill

African Grey Hornbill ☐

Black-and-white Casqued Hornbill ☐

Crowned Hornbill ☐

Red-billed Hornbill ☐

Silvery-cheeked Hornbill ☐

Southern Ground Hornbill ☐

Trumpeter Hornbill ☐

Von der Decken's Hornbill ☐

Red-billed Hornbill

Southern Ground Hornbill

Trumpeter Hornbill

Von der Decken's Hornbill

Hornbills have horn-shaped, curved bills and feed on fruit, berries and some species of insects. They feed by taking the food in the tip of the bill, toss it into the air and swallow it. They drink in the same way, dipping the bill in water, tossing and catching an individual drop in the mouth.

Tinkerbirds   86

Tinkerbirds are also known as tinker-barbets. They are large-headed with a stout bill and are usually strongly marked. Their wings are short and rounded, producing noisy flight.

Moustached Green Tinkerbird ☐

Red-fronted Tinkerbird ☐

Yellow-rumped Tinkerbird ☐

Barbets   87

Crested Barbet

Black-billed Barbet ☐

Black-throated Barbet ☐

Crested Barbet ☐

D'Arnaud's Barbet ☐

Double-toothed Barbet ☐

Red-and-yellow Barbet ☐

Red-fronted Barbet ☐

Spotted-flanked Barbet ☐

Usimbiro Barbet ☐

White-headed Barbet ☐

D'Arnaud's Barbet

Woodpeckers   88

Bearded Woodpecker

Bearded Woodpecker ☐

Bennet's Woodpecker ☐

Brown-backed Woodpecker ☐

Cardinal Woodpecker ☐

Golden-tailed Woodpecker ☐

Green-backed Woodpecker ☐

BIRDS

Bird check list

Grey Woodpecker ☐

Nubian Woodpecker ☐

Woodpeckers have extremely long and mobile tongues which they use to probe under the bark of trees. They have thick skulls and powerful neck muscles to withstand the hammering.

Cardinal Woodpecker

Golden-tailed Woodpecker

Nubian Woodpecker

89 Broadbills

It is a thickset, arboreal forest bird with a large head and broad, flat bill.

African Broadbill ☐

90 Honeyguides

Honeyguides are the only known birds able to digest bees wax. They guide humans or honey badgers to a nest by flight display and chirring noises. Their skins are extra tough to withstand stings.

Greater Honeyguide ☐

Lesser Honeyguide ☐

Scaly-throated Honeyguide ☐

Wahlberg's Honeyguide ☐

91 Larks

African Short-toed Lark (Red-capped Lark)

Crested Lark

African Short-toed Lark/Red-capped Lark ☐

African Singing Bushlark ☐

Crested Lark ☐

Fawn-coloured Lark ☐

Flappet Lark ☐

Short-tailed Lark ☐

Somali Short-toed Lark ☐

Rufous-naped Lark ☐

White-tailed Bushlark ☐

African Larks all have beautiful songs. The African species are terrestrial with plainly-coloured plumage. The back is scaled and not plain like the pipits. All species nest on the ground but they do perch on trees and posts as well. Their diet is largely insects but some feed on seeds also.

Rufous-naped Lark

Sparrow-larks 92

Chestnut-backed Sparrow-lark

Chestnut-backed Sparrow-lark ☐

Fischer's Sparrow-lark ☐

Sparrow-larks or Finch-larks are small birds that breed in semi-arid habitats with sparse ground cover. They nest in an open cup in a scrape in the ground.

Pipits 93

Richard's Pipit

Bush Pipit ☐

Long-billed Pipit ☐

Red-throated Pipit ☐

Richard's Pipit ☐

Tree Pipit ☐

Swallows 94

Rufous-breasted Swallow

Wire-tailed Swallow

Angola Swallow ☐

Barn Swallow ☐

Grey-rumped Swallow ☐

Mosque Swallow ☐

Lesser-striped Swallow ☐

Red-rumped Swallow ☐

Rufous-breasted Swallow ☐

White-tailed Swallow ☐

Wire-tailed Swallow ☐

Swallows have broad bills with wide gapes used as insect traps.

BIRDS

Bird check list

95 Martins

Martins are perching birds that have developed an aerial way of feeding. Their legs are short and weak but their wing-muscles are superior.

- Brown-throated Sand-martin ☐
- Common Sand-martin ☐
- Rock Martin ☐
- Western House Martin ☐

96 Saw-wings

Saw-wings are actually swallows and feed on insects whilst in flight.

- Black Saw-wing ☐
- White-headed Saw-wing ☐

97 Longclaws

Rosy-breasted Longclaw

Yellow-throated Lonclaw

- Pangani Longclaw ☐
- Rosy-breasted Longclaw ☐
- Yellow-throated Longclaw ☐

Longclaws are grassland birds of water-logged areas, spending much time on the ground. Their feet are stout and the hind claw is very long. They are related to wagtails and pipits. They often mount grass tussocks to look around. Their nests are neatly lined cups, often at the base of a grass tuft and are well concealed. The tail of the Rosy-breasted Longclaw is longer than that of other longclaws.

98 Wagtails

African Pied Wagtail

Yellow Wagtail

- African Pied Wagtail ☐
- Grey Wagtail ☐
- Mountain Wagtail ☐
- Yellow Wagtail ☐

Wagtails are monogamous and probably pair for life. They are aggressively territorial. Both build the nest and the male offers nest-building material to the female any time of the year to maintain the bond. Both tend to the chicks. The Pied Wagtail breeds in Africa but the Yellow Wagtail is a palaearctic migrant.

Cuckooshrikes 99

Cuckooshrikes are related to drongos and have no affinities with either shrikes or cuckoos. They have a slight terminal hook on the rather small bill.

- Black Cuckooshrike ☐
- Grey-throated Cuckooshrike ☐
- Purple-throated Cuckooshrike ☐

Bulbuls 100

Common Bulbul

Yellow-bellied Bulbul

- Common Bulbul ☐
- Yellow-bellied Bulbul ☐

Except for the Common Bulbul, which is quite bold, others in this group, like the greenbuls, are rather secretive. The Yellow-bellied Bulbul is confined to thick undergrowth in forests and is very shy. The Common Bulbul occurs almost everywhere except above 3 000m. Plumage is soft with long lower back feathers and hair-like feathers on the nape. They feed on fruit, insects and nectar. The nest is a flimsy cup. Parental care by both sexes.

Greenbuls 101

Greenbuls are very shy birds.

- Olive Mountain Greenbul ☐

Wheatears 102

Capped Wheatear

- Capped Wheatear ☐
- Isabeline Wheatear ☐
- Mourning Wheatear ☐
- Northern Wheatear ☐
- Pied Wheatear ☐

Thrushes 103

Kurrichane Thrush

- Bare-eyed Thrush ☐
- Common Rock-thrush ☐
- Kurrichane Thrush ☐
- Olive Thrush ☐
- Spotted Morning-thrush ☐

BIRDS

Thrushes are ground birds, occuring solitary or in pairs. They run for a few paces, stop, turn their heads and literally listen for insect movement below the soil surface. They feed on insects, mollusks, spiders and lizards. They nest in tree-forks and nests are lined with mud.

Olive Thrush

Robin-chats are monogamous, territorial and they pair for life. They maintain their territory throughout the year. The Cape and Heuglin's Robin-chats are both parasitised by the Red-chested Cuckoo. They have both adapted well to gardens.

Heuglin's Robin-chat

104 — Chats

Alpine Chat	☐
Common Stonechat	☐
Familiar Chat	☐
Irania (Chat)	☐
Mocking Cliff Chat	☐
Northern Ant-eating Chat	☐
Whinchat	☐

Common Stonechat

Mocking Cliff Chat

Chats do not migrate, some make minor movements. All are monogamous and territorial. Chat males show off white patches in their plumage to attract females. Most chats have their nests on the ground under a rock. They build a base of stones, earth, bark, with a small cup for the actual nest. The Ant-eating Chat nests in the walls of Aardvark, Porcupine and Hyena dens and the tunnel to the nest is just under one metre long. The nest itself is also cup-shaped.

Northern Ant-eating Chat

105 — Robins

The bills of robins are slender for picking up insects.

White-browed Scrub-robin	☐
White-starred Robin	☐

106 — Robin-chats

The Cape Robin-chat can be distinguished from the Heuglin's Robin-chat by a shorter white eyebrow and by the greyish-white underparts. They occur in forest edges and are common garden visitors.

Cape Robin-chat	☐
White-browed Robin-chat	☐
Heuglin's Robin-chat	☐
Red-capped Robin-chat	☐
Rueppell's Robin-chat	☐

107 — Blackcaps

The Blackcap is a Warbler with a black cap.

Blackcap (Warbler)	☐

108 — Camaropteras

The Common Camaroptera is also known as the Grey-backed Bleating Warbler.

Common Camaroptera (Warbler)	☐

109 — Warblers

Grey-backed Bleating Warbler

Warblers are extremely vocal, skulking and elusive with small slender bills to eat insects. They are mostly identified by their calls which they use to advertise their territories, maintaining the pair bond for courtship. The Bleating Warbler is unmistakable by its bleat-like call, it also emits a repeated chitip-chitip and produces a trip sound with its wings. Nests consist of growing leaves sewn together with spider web, by pinching holes in the leaves and threading them together with short lengths of spider web.

African Reed Warbler	☐
Brown Warbler	☐
Buff-bellied Warbler	☐
Eurasian Reed Warbler	☐
Garden Warbler	☐
Great Reed Warbler	☐
Grey-backed Bleating Warbler	☐
Grey Bush-warbler	☐
Icterine Warbler	☐
Lesser Swamp Warbler	☐
Miomobo Bush-warbler	☐
Olivaceous Warbler	☐
Olive Tree Warbler	☐
Red-faced Warbler	☐
Sedge Warbler	☐
Willow Warbler	☐

110 — Whitethroats

Common Whitethroat	☐

111 — Cisticolas

Cisticolas can be described as grass warblers because of their preference for grassy habitats in open veld and near streams. They are russet on top, streaked with black and characteristically pale to cream below. They are small birds and the tail is often cocked up. They are mostly seen hanging on grass stems looking for insects. They construct bottle-shaped nests. Cisticolas are known as the most frustrating 'little brown jobs' because they all look similar and have three different plumages - juvenile, breeding and non-breeding. Their name refers to the sound they make.

- Ashy Cisticola ☐
- Croaking Cisticola ☐
- Desert Cisticola ☐
- Pectoral-patch Cisticola ☐
- Rattling Cisticola ☐
- Red-faced Cisticola ☐
- Rock-loving Cisticola ☐
- Siffling Cisticola ☐
- Stout Cisticola ☐
- Trilling Cisticola ☐
- Winding Cisticola ☐
- Wing-snapping Cisticola ☐
- Zitting Cisticola ☐

112 — Prinias

They can be recognised by cocked-up tails.

- Tawny-flanked Prinia ☐

113 — Apalis

The Apalis occurs in all levels of forests and they feed on insects, usually caterpillars. The Apalis is a Warbler.

- Chestnut-throated Apalis ☐
- Grey-capped Apalis ☐
- Yellow-breasted Apalis ☐

114 — Sylvietta/Crombec

They have very short tails and curved bills.

- Red-faced Sylvietta/Crombec ☐

115 — Eremomelas

It is a Warbler with a short tail and yellow belly.

- Yellow-bellied Eremomela ☐

116 — Parisomas

The Banded Parisoma is a warbler with a dark band on its chest.

- Brown Parisoma ☐
- Banded Parisoma ☐

117 — Flycatchers

Pallid Flycatcher

Spotted Flycatcher

- African Dusky Flycatcher ☐
- Collared Flycatcher ☐
- Grey Flycatcher ☐
- Northern Black Flycatcher ☐
- Pallid Flycatcher ☐
- Spotted Flycatcher ☐
- Southern Black Flycatcher ☐
- Swamp Flycatcher ☐
- White-eyed Slaty Flycatcher ☐

118 — Batis

It has a prominent chest band and yellow eyes.

- Chin-spot Batis ☐

119 — Silverbird

Silverbird

- Silverbird ☐

The Silverbird is very common along the Seronera River. It is really a flycatcher with a distinct silver-grey back and tawny-orange underparts. It has a broad-based triangular bill. It is insectivorous, doing much of its feeding in the air.

120 — Wattle-eyes

They can be recognised by the 'wattle' around their eyes.

- Banded Wattle-eye ☐
- Black-throated Wattle-eye ☐

121 — Monarchs

Paradise Monarch (female)

- African Paradise Monarch ☐
- Blue Monarch ☐
- White-tailed Crested Monarch ☐

The Paradise Monarch male chases after the female, flaunting his long tail during courtship. The nest is a very neat, lichen-covered cup.

Paradise Monarch (male)

BIRDS

167

Bird check list

122 Babblers

Arrow-marked Babbler

- African Hill-babbler ☐
- Arrow-marked Babbler ☐
- Black-lored Babbler ☐
- Pied Babbler ☐

123 Chatterers

- Rufous Chatterer ☐

124 Tits

Tits are very acrobatic and may hang upside down as they forage for insects and larvae on twigs.

- African Penduline Tit ☐
- Red-throated Tit ☐
- White-bellied Black Tit ☐

125 White-eyes

Montaine White-eye

- Abyssinian White-eye ☐
- Montaine White-eye ☐

They are monogamous, pair for life, non-territorial and gregarious. Pairs roost seperately. Can be recognised by white ring around eye.

126 Sunbirds

Malachite Sunbird

Variable Sunbird

- Amethyst Sunbird ☐
- Beautiful Sunbird ☐
- Bronze Sunbird ☐
- Collared Sunbird ☐
- Copper Sunbird ☐
- Eastern Double-collared Sunbird ☐
- Eastern Violet-backed Sunbird ☐
- Golden-winged Sunbird ☐
- Malachite Sunbird ☐
- Marico Sunbird ☐

Sunbirds have long, curved bills with which they probe open blossoms or pierce the bases of tubular flowers to get to the nectaries. They have very long, tubular tongues which are split at the end for sipping the nectar.

- Olive Sunbird ☐
- Red-chested Sunbird ☐
- Scarlet-chested Sunbird ☐
- Scarlet-tufted Sunbird ☐
- Variable Sunbird ☐

127 Orioles

Black-headed Oriole

- African Black-headed Oriole ☐
- African Golden Oriole ☐
- Eurasian Oriole ☐

Orioles are known for their clear, liquid calls 'poodleeoo - poodleeoo'. They feed on caterpillars and other insects but will also eat berries.

128 Puffback Shrikes

The male fluffs white rump plumes during courtship

- Black-backed Puffback Shrike ☐

129 Boubou Shrikes

The Boubou Shrikes usually occur in pairs and they call in a duet. They occur along streams or river edges.

- Slate-coloured Boubou (Shrike) ☐
- Tropical Boubou (Shrike) ☐

130 Brubru Shrikes

The Brubru prefers canopies of woodland.

- Brubru (Shrike) ☐

131 Chagra Shrikes

Black-crowned Chagra

- Black-crowned Chagra (Shrike) ☐
- Brown-crowned Chagra (Shrike) ☐
- Marsh Chagra (Shrike) ☐

Chagras are territorial, monogamous and they pair for life. They have elaborate courtship displays in which they spread their tail feathers to reveal the white outer ring.

Brown-crowned Chagra

Bird check list

132   Fiscal Shrikes

Common Fiscal ☐

Grey-backed Fiscal (Shrike) ☐

Long-tailed Fiscal (Shrike) ☐

Taita Fiscal (Shrike) ☐

Common Fiscal

Grey-backed Fiscal   *Taita Fiscal*

133   Shrikes

Black-fronted Bush-shrike ☐

Lesser Grey Shrike ☐

Magpie Shrike ☐

Red-backed Shrike ☐

Red-tailed Shrike ☐

Magpie Shrike

Sulphur-breasted Bush-shrike ☐

White Helmet shrike ☐

Northern White-crowned Shrike ☐

Northern White-crowned Shrike

All Shrikes are predatory birds with hooked bills. They make a cup-shaped nest and often use cobwebs.

Red-backed Swike

134   Crows

Pied Crow ☐

The crow is smaller than a raven, with a thinner bill, and larger than a Cape Rook. They usually scavenge and are often found near human habitation.

Pied Crow

135   Rooks

Cape Rook/Black Crow ☐

The Cape Rook is smaller than the Pied Crow and less of a scavenger. They feed mainly on insects, frogs, fruits and grain. They tame well and make good pets.

Cape Rook

136   Ravens

White-naped Raven ☐

It can be recognised by a heavy bill and occurs from 400m to 4 000m above sea level and is therefore very widespread. It mainly scavenges.

White-naped Raven

137   Starlings

Ashy Starling ☐

Greater Blue-eared Starling ☐

Hildebrandt's Starling ☐

Purple-headed Starling ☐

Red-winged Starling ☐

Greater Blue-eared Starling

Rueppell's Long-tailed Starling ☐

Sharpe's Starling ☐

Superb Starling ☐

Violet-backed Starling ☐

Superb Starling

Waller's Starling ☐

Wattled Starling ☐

Wattled Starling

Red-winged Starlings stay together all year, so there is no need for courtship. Wattled starlings are nomadic, sociable and breed opportunistically when conditions are right. They build very large dome-shaped nests with a side entrance, much different to other starlings. The Red-winged starling nest colonially in 1-1,5 m deep holes in river banks.

Violet-backed Starling

B I R D S

138   Drongos

African Drongo ☐

Drongos are monogamous and aggressively territorial, chasing raptors relentlessly, even clinging to their backs and pecking them in flight. Their nests are placed hammock-like in the fork of a horizontal branch.

African Drongo

139   Oxpeckers

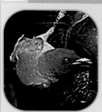

Red-billed Oxpecker ☐

Yellow-billed Oxpecker ☐

Oxpecker populations have declined since cattle dipping has deprived them of their staple diet - ticks. Their bills are flattened on the side, enabling them to shear the ticks from the animal's hide.

Red-billed Oxpecker

140   Sparrows

Grey-headed Sparrow ☐

Chestnut Sparrow ☐

Rufous Sparrow ☐

Sparrows are granivorous, ground-feeding birds of open country. They build untidy, domed nests with side entrances.

Malachite Sunbird

141   Weavers

Black-headed Weaver ☐

Black-necked Weaver ☐

Chestnut Weaver ☐

Grey-headed Social Weaver ☐

Grosbeak Weaver ☐

Grey-headed Social Weaver

Golden-backed Weaver ☐

Large Golden Weaver ☐

Lesser Masked Weaver ☐

Little Weaver ☐

Parasitic Weaver ☐

Lesser Masked Weaver

Red-billed Buffalo Weaver ☐

Red-headed Weaver ☐

Rufous-tailed Weaver ☐

Speckled Weaver ☐

Speckle-fronted Weaver ☐

Slender-billed Weaver ☐

Speke's Weaver ☐

Vitelline Masked Weaver ☐

White-headed Buffalo Weaver ☐

Red-billed Buffalo Weaver

Rufous-tailed Weaver

Most Weavers are parasitised by the Diederik Cuckoo.

Vitelline Masked Weaver

Red-headed Weaver

Speckled Weaver

White-headed Buffalo Weaver

Malimbas   142

This is a black bird with a red head.

Red-headed Malimba (Weaver) ☐

Widowbirds   143

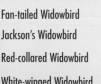

Fan-tailed Widowbird ☐

Jackson's Widowbird ☐

Red-collared Widowbird ☐

White-winged Widowbird ☐

Females are short-tailed and dull.

Fan-tailed Widowbird

Bird check list

Male widowbirds develop prominent tails, they turn black and have coloured shoulders. After breeding they become dull, like the females. They have spherical, woven nests with side entrances, which are placed low in grass tufts or shrubs.

White-winged Widowbird

The Southern Cordon Bleu is also known as the Blue Waxbill. They breed in association with social wasps, but the reason is not certain. It has been suggested that wasps choose trees free of *Acacia* ants because the ants prey on their larvae. This association frees the birds of ants in the nest.

Southern Cordon Bleu

144   Bishops

Black Bishop	☐
Southern Red Bishop	☐
Yellow Bishop	☐
Yellow-crowned Bishop	☐

Southern Red Bishop

149   Crimsonwings

They occur in highland forest clearings.

Abyssinian Crimsonwing	☐

150   Cut-throat Finches

The male has a red band across the throat.

Cut-throat Finch	☐

145   Queleas/Finches

Cardinal Quelea	☐
Red-billed Quelea	☐
Red-headed Quelea	☐

Queleas occur in flocks of millions and they feed on dry grass seeds, causing major damage to crops.

Red-billed Quelea

151   Firefinches

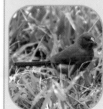

African Firefinch	☐
Red-billed Firefinch	☐

They often occur on the ground and feed on grass seeds. Their colouration varies from red to maroon to brown.

Red-billed Firefinch

146   Whydahs

Breeding male wydahs develop long tail feathers. They are host-specific brood-parasites on Waxbills. They do not evict the host chicks and maintain a bond with the host parents for some time.

Acacia Paradise Whydah	☐
Straw-coloured Whydah	☐
Pin-tailed Whydah	☐
Steel-blue Whydah	☐

152   Grenadiers

Purple Grenadier	☐

Grenadiers are common in bush and are often on or near the ground. They feed on grass seeds. Their chicks have reflective tubercles at the side of the mouth indicating the position of the mouth in the dark nest. They have purple markings on the side of the head.

Purple Grenadier

147   Blackfinches

Grey-crowned Blackfinch	☐

153   Indigo Birds

They are parasitised by Firefinches

Village Indigobird	☐

148   Cordon Bleus

Blue-capped Cordon Bleu	☐
Red-cheeked Cordon Bleu	☐
Southern Cordon Bleu	☐

Only the male of the Red-cheeked Cordon Bleu has red cheeks.

Red-cheeked Cordon Bleu

154   Mannikins

The Bronze Mannikin builds a brooding nest in winter, separate from the breeding nest.

Bicoloured Mannikin	☐
Bronze Mannikin	☐

Bird check list

155 Oriole-finches

They have black heads and yellow bodies.
Oriole-finch ☐

156 Pytilias

Green-winged Pytilias ☐

Green-winged Pytilias

The Green-winged Pytilia is also known as the Melba Finch and is host to the Paradise Whydah. It finds most of its food (termites, seeds) on the ground. It favours areas of dense, low *Acacia* thickets, *A. tortilis* being a favourite.

157 Quailfinches

African Quailfinch ☐

158 Silverbills

They can be recognised by their grey heads and silver bills.
African Silverbill ☐
Grey-headed Silverbill ☐

159 Twinspots

Green Twinspot ☐

160 Waxbills

Waxbills have strong, conical bills suited to cracking and de-husking seeds. Food in the crops of birds is enriched by the addition of protein secretions before it is fed to the young. They are monogamous and mate for life. They reinforce the bond by mutual preening and huddling.

Black-cheeked Waxbill ☐
Black-faced Waxbill ☐
Common Waxbill ☐
Crimson-rumped Waxbill ☐
Fawn-breasted Waxbill ☐
Yellow-bellied Waxbill ☐

161 Buntings

Buntings can be distinguished from finches by their wavy-edged upper mandible.
Cinnamon-breasted Rock Bunting ☐
Golden-breasted Bunting ☐

162 Canaries

Yellow-fronted Canary

Yellow-crowned Canary ☐
Yellow-fronted Canary ☐

All canaries line their cup-shaped nests with downy plant material, usually white in colour. They are fine songsters and have regular song perches. Canary nests remain clean as faecal sacs are removed or eaten.

163 Citrils

African Citril ☐

164 Serins

Serins are closely related to canaries. The Grosbeak Serin has a thick bill.
Grosbeak Serin ☐
Streaky Serin ☐

Did You Know?

- The male Sandgrouse has specially adapted feathers that can absorb water, which is carried back to the chicks in the nest. The feathers have barbules that uncoil when they come into contact with water. These microscopic filaments soak up the water by capillary action. They can soak up to 22ml of water, of which about half or two thirds will make it to the nest. (Steyn, 1996).

- A flock of White Helmet-shrikes has a single breeding pair and all members assist in incubation, feeding the chicks and tending to sanitation of the nest. At sexual maturity a group of brothers may team up with a group of sisters from a another flock to form a new flock.

- Snake Eagles feed almost exclusively on snakes. The Brown Snake Eagle hunts from a perch and the Black-breasted Snake Eagle hunts on the wing. They both drop the snake to stun it and then sieze it again, swallowing it whole - head first. When they take snake prey to their chicks, they allow them to pull it out of their crop. The parent may assist the chick by pulling the snake out with its talons (claws). The chick can swallow up to a metre length at one time.

- Quelea Finches are the most abundant land birds in Africa. Their breeding is highly synchronised and is determined by protein levels in their blood. They will only breed if there is sufficient fresh grass seeds and larvae to feed their chicks. They have the shortest breeding cycle of all birds. Mating and nest-building takes ±10-12 days, even though they have to do ±700 round trips to collect material. They lay ±3 eggs over two days and each egg requires only ±30 hours for hatching. The young leave the nest at 11-13 days. The whole cycle may be only 35 days. The snake-like flocks that they form may represent about one million individuals and the continues streams, up to five million birds. They have a great economic impact on commercial crops.

CONTACT DETAILS

Contact details of safari companies, lodges and airline companies

Hotels and lodges in Arusha

Impala Hotel
Tel: + 255 27 250-8448 / 8449 / 8450 / 8451
Fax: +255 27 250-8220 / 8680
E-mail: impala@cybernet.co.tz
or impala@habari.co.tz
Website: www.impalahotel.com

Kibo Palace
Tel: + 255 27 254-4945/4624
Fax: +255 27 254-8832
E-mail: info@kibopalacehotel.com
Website: www.kibopalacehotel.com

Le Jacaranda
Tel: + 255 27 254-4472
Fax: +255 27 254-8585
E-mail: jacaranda@tz2000.com
Website: www.chez.com/jacaranda

Masai Camp (camping and rooms)
Tel (mobile): + 255 744-898-800
E-mail: masaicamp.com

Ngurdoto Mountain Lodge (Usa-River)
Tel: + 255 27 255-5217 / 18 / 19 / 20 / 21 / 22 / 23 / 24 / 25 / 26
Fax: +255 27 255-5227/5228
E-mail: ngurdoto@thengurdotomountainlodge.com
Website: www.thengurdotomountainlodge.com

Arumeru River Lodge (Usa-River)
Tel: + 255 27 255-3573
Fax: + 255 27 255-3574
Mobile: +255 (0) 748-459-649
E-mail: info@arumerulodge.com

Hotels and lodges in near Ngorongoro

CC Africa (CONSCORP LTD)
Klein's Camp
Grumeti River Camp
Ngorongoro Crater Lodge
Lake Manyara Tree Lodge
Tel: +255 27 254-8078 / 5849
Fax: + 255 27 254-4058
Tel SA: +27 11 809-4300
Fax SA: +27 11 809-4400
E-mail: information @ccafrica.com or
arusha@ccafrica.co.tz
Website: www.ccafrica.com

Hotels and Lodges
Lobo Wildlife Lodge
Ngorongoro Wildlife Lodge
Serena Wildlife Lodge
Tel: + 255 27 254-4595
Fax: + 255 27 254-8633
E-mail: liaison@hotelsandlodges-tanzania.com
or control@hotelsandlodges-tanzania.com
Website: www.hotelsandlodges-tanzania.com

Sopa Lodges & Elewana Africa
Serengeti Sopa Lodge
Ngorongoro Sopa Lodge
Tel: +255 27 250-0630
E-mail: info@sopalodges.com
Website: www.sopalodges.com or
www.elewana.com

Abercrombie & Kent / Sanctuary Lodges
Kusini Camp
Swala Camp
Tel: +255 27 250-9816 / 7
Fax: + 255 27 250-8237
E-mail: tanzania@sanctuarylodges.com
Website: www.sanctuarylodges.com

Serena Hotels
Kirawira Serena Tented Camp
Serengeti Serena Lodge
Ngorongoro Serena Lodge
Tel: +255 22 250-8175
Fax: + 255 27 250-4155
E-mail: dmkina@serena.co.tz
Website: www.serenahotels.com

Kibo Safaris
Ngorongoro Farm House
Tel: + 255 27 250-7605 / 4093
Fax: + 255 27 250-8937
Mobile: +255 (0) 748 507 605
E-mail: kibosaf@habari.co.tz or
wildwilly@habari.co.tz
Website: www.kibo-safaris.com

Kudu Lodge and Campsite (Karatu area)
Tel: + 255 27 253-4268/4055/4412
Fax: + 255 27 253-4268
Mobile: +255 (0) 744 474 792
E-mail: kuducamp@iwayafrica.com
or dawsongm@yahoo.com
Website: www.kuducamp.com

Ndutu Safari Lodge (at Lake Ndutu)
Tel: + 255 27 250-6702/2829
Fax: + 255 27 250-8310
E-mail: bookings@ndutu.com or info@ndutu.com
Website: www.ndutu.com

Tarangire Safari Lodge
Tel: + 255 27 254-4595
Fax: + 255 27 254-8633
E-mail: tarsaf@habari.co.tz /
info@emayanilodge.com /sss@habari.co.tz
Website: www.tarangiresafarilodge.com /
www.emayanilodge.com

Gibb's Farm
Tel: +255 27 253-4040
E-mail: bas.gibbs@habari.co.tz
Website: www.gibbsfarm.net

Safari Companies in Arusha

Bobby Camping Safaris
Tel: + 255 27 254-4057/4058
Fax: + 255 27 254-4057
Mobile: +255 (0) 744-311-471 or (0) 744-262-925
E-mail: bobbycamping@yako.habari.co.tz /
bobbycamping@habari.co.tz
Website: www.habari.co.tz/bobbycamping or
www.bobbycamping.com

Bushbuck Safaris
Tel: + 255 27 250-7779 /
254-4186 / 4308 / 8924 / 8939
Fax: + 255 27 254-8293 / 4860
E-mail: bushbuck@bushbuckltd.com
Website: www.bushbuckltd.com

Fortes Safaris Ltd.
Tel: + 255 27 250-8096
Mobile: + 255 (0) 744-397-628
E-mail: arushafortes@habari.co.tz

Hoopoe Safaris
Tel: +255 27 250-7011
E-mail: information @hoopoe.com
Website: www.hoopoe.com

J.M. Tours Ltd.
Tel: + 255 27 250-1086 / 1034
Fax: + 255 27 250-1034
Mobile: +255 (0) 744-481-453
E-mail: jmtours@habari.co.tz
Website: www.jmtours.co.tz

Ker & Downey Safaris
Tel: + 255 27 250-8917
Fax: +255 27 250-8434
Mobile: +255 (0) 748-507-605
E-mail: belinda.ambrose@tgts.com
or charl.beukes@tgts.com

Kibo Safaris
Tel: + 255 27 250-7605 / 4093
Fax: + 255 27 250-8937
Mobile: +255 (0) 748 507 605
E-mail: kibosaf@habari.co.tz or
wildwilly@habari.co.tz
Website: www.kibo-safaris.com

Kudu Safaris
Tel: + 255 27 250-6065 / 8193
Fax: + 255 27 254-8298
Mobile: +255 (0) 748 507 605
E-mail: kudu@habari.co.tz

Macho Ya Tanzania Ltd.
Tel: + 255 27 253-4268/4055
Fax: + 255 27 253-4268
E-mail: dawson.minja@macho-ya-tanzania.com
or macho-ya-tanzania@iwayafrica.com
Website: www.macho-ya-tanzania.com

Leopard Tours
Tel: + 255 27 250-4610 / 4611 / 4612 /
4613 / 7906 / 3603
Fax: + 255 27 250-4131 / 4134 / 8219
E-mail: leopard@yako.co.tz
Website: www.leopard-tours.com

Mount Kilimanjaro Safari Club
Tel: + 255 27 250-7905
Fax: +255 27 250-8869
E-mail: mksc3@habari.co.tz
Website: www.tanganyika.com

Ranger Safaris Ltd.
Tel: + 255 27 250-3023 / 3074 / 3738
Fax: + 255 27 250-8205 / 8749
E-mail: lalji@rangersafaris.co.tz
Website: www.rangersafaris.com

Roy Safaris
Tel: +255 27 250-7940 / 7057 / 8010
Fax: + 255 27 254-8892
E-mail: RoySafaris@intafrica.com or
Sanjay@roysafaris.com
Website: www.roysafaris.com

Serengeti Select Safaris
Tel: + 255 27 254-4222 / 4752
Tel/Fax: + 255 27 254-4752
Mobile: +255 (0) 748-202-777
E-mail: sss@habari.co.tz
Website: www.serengetisafaris.com

TAWISA
*(See Mount Kilimanjaro
Safari Club)*

Thomson Safaris
Tel: + 255 27 250-8551
Tel USA: + 1 800 235 0289 / 1 617 923 0426
Fax: + 255 27 254-8494
E-mail: tsafari@habari.co.tz
E-mail USA: info@thomsonsafaris.com
Website: www.ThomsonSafaris.com

Tropical Trails
Tel: + 255 27 250-0358/5578
Fax: +255 27 250-5578
E-mail: tropicaltrails@bol.co.tz
Website: www.tropicaltrails.com

Unique Safaris
Tel: + 255 27 255-
3863/3823/3843
Fax: + 255 27 255-3527/3858
E-mail: uniquesaf@cybernet.co.tz
Website: www.uniquesafaris.com

Balloon Safaris / Airline companies

Serengti Balloon Safaris
Tel: +255 27 250-8578 / 8254 / 8967
or +255 748-422- 359
Tel UK: 01379 853 129
Fax: +255 27 254-8997
Fax UK: 01379 853 127
E-mail: balloons@habari.co.tz
E-mail UK: cirrus@flyingjacket.com
Website: www.balloonsafaris.com /
www.flyingjacket.com
BASED: At Seronera in the Serengeti National Park

Air Excel Ltd
Tel / Fax: +255 27 250-1595 / 1597 / 254-8429
Mobile: +255 (0) 741-510-857 or (0) 744-211-227
E-mail: reservations @airexcelonline.com

Air Tanzania Company Ltd
Tel: +255 27 250-3201
Fax: + 255 27 254-4058
E-mail: airtanzania-ark@cybernet.co.tz
Website: www.airtanzania.com

Northern Air
Tel: +255 27 250-8059/60
E-mail: northernair@habari.co.tz

Precision Air Services Ltd
Tel: +255 27 250-6903/2836/7319
E-mail: information@precisionairtz.com
pwmarketing@precisionairtz.com
pwreservations@precisionairtz.com
Website: www.precisionairtz.com

Parks and Reserves / Government Organisations

Tanzania National Parks
Tel: +255 27 250-1930
Fax: +255 27 250-8216
E-mail: tanapa@yako.habari.co.tz
Website: www.tanapa.com
BASED: In Arusha

Tanzania Tourist Board (TTB)
Tel: +255 22 254-4754/5
E-mail:
sss@habari.co.tz or tarsaf@habari.co.tz
Website: www.tanzaniatouristboard.com

Ngorongoro Conservation Area Authority
Tel (Arusha): +255 27 250-3339 or 254-4625
Tel (Ngorongoro): +255 27 253-7019 / 7006 / 7046
Fax (Arusha): +255 27 254-8752
Fax (Ngorongoro): +255 27 253-7007
E-mail: ncaa_faru@cybernet.co.tz
or ncaa_info@cybernet.co.tz
or ncaa-info@africaonline.co tz
Website: www.ngorongoro-crater-africa.org
BASED: In Arusha and at the Ngororongoro Crater

The author does not take responsiblity for any changes in contact details

Car Hire

Fortes Car Hire
E-mail: wendy@fortes-safaris.com
Website: www.fortescarhire.com

Avis Rent A Car
Tel. Arusha: +255 27 250-9108
E-mail Arusha: skylink.arusha@cybernet.co.tz
Website: www.skylinktanzania.com

BIBLIOGRAPHY

BLUNDELL, M. 1992. *Wild flowers of East Africa.* Harper Collins Publishers.

CILLIE, B. 1997. *The Mammals Guide of South Africa.* Briza Publications, PO Box 56569, Arcadia, 0007, Pretoria, South Africa.

DHARANI, N. 2002. *Field Guide to Common Trees and Shrubs of East Africa.* Struik Publishers.

ESTES, R. 1991. *The Behavior Guide to African Mammals.* University of California Press, Ltd.

HANBY, J & BYGOTT, D. 1999. *Ngorongoro Conservation Area.* Kibuyu Partners, PO Box 161, Karatu, Tanzania.

HALTENORTH, T & DILLER, H. 1992. *Mammals of Africa including Madagascar.* Collins, London.

HERLOCKER, D. 1973. *Woody Vegetation of the Serengeti National Park.*

The Caesar Kleberg Research Program in Wildlife Ecology. IUCN, 1996. *Management Zone Plan.* **Serengeti National Park, Tanzania.**

KINGDON, J. 1997. *The Kingdon Field Guide to African Mammals.* Academic Press, San Diego.

LIVERSEDGE, R. 1991. *The Birds Around Us.* Fontein Publishing Company Limited, PO Box 967 Parklands, 2121, South Africa.

MARTIN, D. 2000. *Serengeti & Tanzania, Land, People, History.* African Publishing Group, PO Box BW 350, Harare, Zimbabwe. Tanzania Natonal Park, PO Box 3134, Arusha, Tanzania.

MARTIN. D. 2000. *Ngorongoro, Land, People, History.* African Publishing Group, PO Box BW 350, Harare, Zimbabwe. Ngorongoro Conservation Area Authority, PO Box 1, Ngorongoro, Tanzania

NCAA, 1991. *A Tourism Management Plan.* United Republic of Tanzania.

NCAA, 1994. *Ngorongoro's Geological History.* The Ngorongoro Conservation Area Authority, PO Box 1, Ngorongoro Crater, Arusha, Tanzania

NCAA, 1994. *Ngorongoro's Animal Life.* The Ngorongoro Conservation Area Authority, PO Box 1, Ngorongoro Crater, Arusha, Tanzania

NELSON, D & BYGOTT, D. 1992. *Serengeti National Park.* TANAPA, PO Box 3134, Arusha, Tanzania

NEWMAN, K. 1979. *Birdlife in South Africa.* Macmillan South Africa Limited, Johannesburg.

NOAD, D. & BIRNIE. A. 1992. *Trees of Kenya.* T.C. Noad and A. Birnie. PO Box 40034, Nairobi, Kenya.

PARKER,S., 1992. *The Dawn of Man.* Quarto Publishing. The Old Brewery, 6, Blundell Street, London N7 9BH.

ROODT, V. 1998. *Common Wild Flowers of the Okavango Delta.* Shell Oil Botswana. PO Box 334, Gaborone, Botswana.

ROODT, V. 1998. *Trees and Shrubs of the Okavango Delta.* Shell Oil Botswana. PO Box 334, Gaborone, Botswana.

STEYN, P. 1996. *Nesting Birds.* Fernwood Press, PO Box 15344, 8118, Vlaeberg.

ZIMMERMAN, TURNER & PEARSON, 1999. *Birds of Kenya & Northern Tanzania.* Christopher Helm (Publishers) Ltd. Bedford Row, London WC1R 4JH.

Giraffe drinking water

INDEX

Take note: To look up a certain species of animal, plant, bird, tribe, rock type, etc, refer to the main group in which it occurs such as Amphibians; Animals; Birds; Butterflies; Grasses; Insects; Medicinal uses of plants; Ngorongoro Crater; Reptiles; Snakes; Trees; Tribes; Wild Flowers. The groups are indicated in bold for easy reference.

177

182